BROKEN THINGS
to Mend

BROKEN
THINGS
to Mend

JEFFREY R. HOLLAND

DESERET
BOOK

SALT LAKE CITY, UTAH

Library of Congress Cataloging-in-Publication Data

Holland, Jeffrey R., 1940-
  Broken things to mend / Jeffrey R. Holland.
     p. cm.
  Includes bibliographical references and index.
  ISBN 978-1-60641-024-0 (hardbound : alk. paper)
  1. Church of Jesus Christ of Latter-day Saints—Doctrines. 2. Mormon
Church—Doctrines. I. Title.
  BX8635.3.H65 2008
  230'.9332—dc22   2008024936

Printed in the United States of America
Publishers Printing, Salt Lake City, UT

10 9 8 7 6 5 4 3 2 1

To all who feel that someone—or something—they love
is irreparably broken or irretrievably lost.
It is not.

CONTENTS

All Things Are Possible

True Prophets and True Principles

The Source of All Healing

STRENGTH FOR THE WEARY SOUL

CHAPTER 1

BROKEN THINGS TO MEND

The first words Jesus spoke in His majestic Sermon on the Mount were to the troubled, the discouraged and down-hearted. "Blessed are the poor in spirit," He said, "for theirs is the kingdom of heaven" (Matthew 5:3). Many people are facing personal trials and family struggles, enduring conflicts fought in the lonely foxholes of the heart, trying to hold back floodwaters of despair that sometimes wash over us like a tsunami of the soul. What follows is especially for those who feel their lives are broken, seemingly beyond repair.

To all such I offer the surest and sweetest remedy that I know. It is found in the clarion call the Savior of the world Himself gave. He said it in the beginning of His ministry, and He said it in the end. He said it to believers, and He said it to those who were not so sure. He said to everyone, whatever their personal problems might be:

"Come unto me, all ye that labour and are heavy laden, and

I will give you rest. Take my yoke upon you, and learn of me; for I am meek and lowly in heart: and ye shall find rest unto your souls" (Matthew 11:28–29).

In this promise, that introductory phrase, "come unto me," is crucial. It is the key to the peace and rest we seek. Indeed, when the resurrected Savior gave His sermon at the temple to the Nephites in the New World, He began, "Blessed are the poor in spirit who *come unto me,* for theirs is the kingdom of heaven" (3 Nephi 12:3; emphasis added).

When Andrew and John first heard Christ speak, they were so moved that they followed Him as He walked away from the crowd. Sensing He was being pursued, Jesus turned and asked the two men, "What seek ye?" They answered, "Where dwellest thou?" And Christ said, "Come and see." The next day He found another disciple, Philip, and said to him, "Follow me" (see John 1:35–39, 43). Just a short time later He formally called Peter and others of the new Apostles with the same spirit of invitation. Come, "follow me," He said (Matthew 4:19).

It seems clear that the essence of our duty, the fundamental requirement of our mortal life, is captured in these brief phrases from any number of scenes in the Savior's mortal ministry. He could have said to us, "Trust me, learn of me, do what I do. Then, when you walk where *I* am going," He says, "we can talk about where *you* are going, and the problems you face and the troubles you have. If you will follow me, I will lead you out of darkness," He promises. "I will give you answers to your prayers. I will give you rest to your souls."

I know of no other way for us to succeed or to be safe amid life's many pitfalls and problems. I know of no other way for us to carry our burdens or find what Jacob in the Book of Mormon called "that happiness which is prepared for the saints" (2 Nephi 9:43).

So how does one "come unto Christ" in response to this constant invitation? The scriptures give scores of examples and avenues. You are well acquainted with the most basic ones. The easiest and the earliest comes simply with the desire of our heart, the most basic form of faith that we know. "If ye can no more than *desire* to believe," Alma says, exercising just "a *particle* of faith," giving even a small place for the promises of God to find a home—that is enough to begin (see Alma 32:27; emphasis added). Just believing, just having a molecule of faith—simply hoping for things which are not yet seen in our lives, but which are nevertheless truly there to be bestowed (see Alma 32:21)—that simple step, when focused on the Lord Jesus Christ, has ever been and always will be the first principle of His eternal gospel, the first step out of despair.

Just believing, just having a molecule of faith . . . when focused on the Lord Jesus Christ, has ever been and always will be the first principle of His eternal gospel, the first step out of despair.

Second, we must change anything we can change that may be part of the problem. In short, we must repent, perhaps the most hopeful and encouraging word in the Christian vocabulary. We thank our Father in Heaven we are *allowed* to change, we thank Jesus we *can* change, and ultimately we do so only with their divine assistance. Certainly not everything we struggle with is a result of our actions. Often our trials result from the actions of others or just the mortal events of life. But anything *we* can change we should change, and we must forgive the rest. In this way our access to the Savior's Atonement becomes as unimpeded as we, with our imperfections, can make it. He will take it from there.

Third, in as many ways as possible we try to take upon us His identity, and we begin by taking upon us His name. That name is formally bestowed by covenant in the saving ordinances of the gospel. These start with baptism and conclude with temple covenants, with many others, such as partaking of the sacrament, laced throughout our lives as additional blessings and reminders. Teaching the people of his day this message, Nephi said: "Follow the Son, with full purpose of heart, . . . with real intent, . . . take upon you the name of Christ. . . . Do the things which I have told you I have seen that your Lord and your Redeemer [will] do" (2 Nephi 31:13, 17).

Following these most basic teachings, a splendor of connections to Christ opens up to us in multitudinous ways: prayer and fasting and meditation upon His purposes, savoring the scriptures, giving service to others, "succor[ing] the weak, lift[ing] up the hands which hang down, . . . strengthen[ing] the feeble knees" (D&C 81:5). Above all else, loving with "the pure love of Christ," that gift that "never faileth," that gift that "beareth all things, believeth all things, hopeth all things, [and] endureth all things" (Moroni 7:47, 46, 45). Soon, with that kind of love, we realize our days hold scores of thoroughfares leading to the Master and that every time we reach out,

Every time we reach out, however feebly, for Him, we discover He has been anxiously trying to reach us.

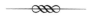

however feebly, for Him, we discover He has been anxiously trying to reach us. So we step, we strive, we seek, and we never yield.[1]

My desire is for all of us—not just those who are "poor in spirit" but all of us—to have more straightforward personal experience with the Savior's example. Sometimes we seek heaven too obliquely, focusing on programs or history or the experience of others. Those are important, but not as important as personal experience, true discipleship, and the strength that comes from experiencing firsthand the majesty of His touch.

Are you battling a demon of addiction—tobacco or drugs or gambling, or the pernicious contemporary plague of pornography? Is your marriage in trouble or your child in danger? Are you struggling with gender issues or searching for self-esteem? Do you—or does someone you love—face disease or depression or death? Whatever other steps you may need to take to resolve these concerns, come first to the gospel of Jesus

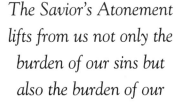

The Savior's Atonement lifts from us not only the burden of our sins but also the burden of our disappointments and sorrows.

Christ. Trust in heaven's promises. In that regard Alma's testimony is my testimony: "I do know," he says, "that whosoever shall put their trust in God shall be supported in their trials, and their troubles, and their afflictions" (Alma 36:3).

This reliance upon the merciful nature of God is at the very center of the gospel Christ taught. I testify that the Savior's Atonement lifts from us not only the burden of our sins but also the burden of our disappointments and sorrows, our heartaches and our despair (see Alma 7:11–12). From the beginning, trust in such help was to give us both a reason and a way to improve, an incentive to lay down our burdens and take up our salvation. There can and will be plenty of difficulties in life. Nevertheless, the soul who comes unto Christ, who knows His voice and strives to do as He did, finds a strength, as the hymn says, "beyond [his] own."[2] The Savior reminds us that He has "graven [us] upon the palms of [His] hands" (1 Nephi 21:16). Considering the incomprehensible cost of the Crucifixion and Atonement, I promise you He is not going to turn His back on us now. When He says to the poor in spirit, "Come unto me," He means He knows the way out and He knows the way up. He knows it because He has walked it. He knows the way because He *is* the way.

Whatever your distress, please don't give up and please don't yield to fear. I have always been touched that as his son was departing for his mission to England, Brother Bryant S. Hinckley gave young Gordon a farewell embrace and then slipped him a handwritten note with just five words taken from the fifth chapter of Mark: "Be not afraid, only believe" (Mark 5:36). I think also of that night when Christ rushed to the aid of His frightened disciples, walking as He did on the water to get to them, calling out, "It is I; be not afraid." Peter exclaimed, "Lord, if it be thou, bid me come unto thee on the water." Christ's answer to him was as it always is, every time: "Come," He said. Instantly, as was his nature, Peter sprang over the vessel's side and into the troubled waters. While his eyes were fixed upon the Lord, the wind could toss his hair and the spray could drench his robes, but all was well—he was coming to Christ. It was only when his faith wavered and fear took control, only when he removed his glance from the Master to look at the furious waves and the ominous black gulf beneath, only then did he begin to sink into the sea. In newer terror he cried out, "Lord, save me."

Undoubtedly with some sadness, the Master over every problem and fear, He who is the solution to every discouragement and disappointment, stretched out His hand and grasped the drowning disciple with the gentle rebuke, "O thou of little faith, *wherefore didst thou doubt?*" (Matthew 14:27–31; emphasis added).

If you are discouraged, please know you can find hope. If you are poor in spirit, please know you can be strengthened.

If you are lonely, please know you can find comfort. If you are discouraged, please know you can find hope. If you are poor in spirit, please know you can be strengthened. If you feel you are broken, please know you can be mended.

> *In Nazareth, the narrow road,*
> *That tires the feet and steals the breath,*
> *Passes the place where once abode*
> *The Carpenter of Nazareth.*
>
> *And up and down the dusty way*
> *The village folk would often wend;*
> *And on the bench, beside Him, lay*
> *Their broken things for Him to mend.*
>
> *The maiden with the doll she broke,*
> *The woman with the broken chair,*
> *The man with broken plough, or yoke,*
> *Said, "Can you mend it, Carpenter?"*

And each received the thing he sought,
In yoke, or plough, or chair, or doll;
The broken thing which each had brought
Returned again a perfect whole.

So, up the hill the long years through,
With heavy step and wistful eye,
The burdened souls their way pursue,
Uttering each the plaintive cry:

"O Carpenter of Nazareth,
This heart, that's broken past repair,
This life, that's shattered nigh to death,
Oh, can You mend them, Carpenter?"

And by His kind and ready hand,
His own sweet life is woven through
Our broken lives, until they stand
A New Creation—"all things new."

"The shattered [substance] of [the] heart,
Desire, ambition, hope, and faith,
Mould Thou into the perfect part,
O, Carpenter of Nazareth!"[3]

May we all, especially the poor in spirit, come unto Him and be made whole.

NOTES

From a talk given at general conference, April 2006.

1. See Alfred Lord Tennyson, "Ulysses," in *The Complete Poetical Works of Tennyson* (1898), 89.

2. "Lord, I Would Follow Thee," in *Hymns of The Church of Jesus Christ of*

Latter-day Saints (Salt Lake City: The Church of Jesus Christ of Latter-day Saints, 1985), no. 220.

3. George Blair, "The Carpenter of Nazareth," in *The Story of Jesus in the World's Literature*, ed. Edward Wagenknecht (Creative Age Press, 1946), 117.

KEEPING FAMILIES WHOLE

CHAPTER 2

A Prayer for the Children

At the close of His first day teaching among the Nephite faithful, the resurrected Jesus turned His attention to a special audience that often stands just below the level of our gaze, sometimes nearly out of sight.

The sacred record says: "He commanded that their little children should be brought [forward]. . . .

"And . . . when they had knelt upon the ground, . . . he himself also knelt . . . ; and behold he prayed unto the Father, and the things which he prayed cannot be written, . . . so great and marvelous [were the] things . . . [He did] speak unto the Father.

" . . . When Jesus had made an end of praying . . . , he arose; . . . and . . . wept, . . . and he took their little children, one by one, and blessed them, and [again] prayed unto the Father for them.

"And when he had done this he wept again; . . . [saying] unto the multitude, . . . Behold your little ones."

We cannot know exactly what the Savior was feeling in such a poignant moment, but we do know that He was "troubled" and that He "groaned within himself" over the destructive influences always swirling around the innocent (3 Nephi 17:11, 14–16, 18, 21–23). We know He felt a great need to pray for and bless the children.

We are not alone, and we do not tremble as if abandoned.

In such times as we are in, whether the threats be global or local or in individual lives, I too pray for the children. Some days it seems that a sea of temptation and transgression inundates them, simply washes over them before they can successfully withstand it, before they should have to face it. And often at least some of the forces at work seem beyond our personal control.

Well, some of them may be beyond our control, but I testify with faith in the living God that they are not beyond His. He lives, and priesthood power is at work on both sides of the veil. We are not alone, and we do not tremble as if abandoned. In doing our part, we can live the gospel and defend its principles. We can declare to others the sure Way, the saving Truth, the joyful Life (see John 14:6). We can personally repent in any way we need to repent, and when we have done all, we can pray. In all these ways we can bless one another and especially those who need our protection the most—the children. As parents we can hold life together the way it is always held together—with love and faith, passed on to the next generation, one child at a time.

In offering such a prayer for the young, may I touch on a rather specific aspect of their safety? In this I address myself carefully and lovingly to any of the adults of the Church, parents or otherwise, who may be given to cynicism or skepticism, who in matters of whole-souled devotion always seem to hang back a little, who at the Church's doctrinal campsite always like to pitch their tents out on the periphery of religious faith. To all such—whom we do love and wish were more comfortable camping nearer to us—I say, please be aware that the full price to be paid for such a stance does not always come due in your lifetime. No, sadly, some elements of this can be a kind of profligate national debt, with payments coming out of your children's and grandchildren's pockets in far more expensive ways than you ever intended it to be.

In this Church there is an enormous amount of room—and scriptural commandment—for studying and learning, for comparing and considering, for discussion and awaiting further revelation. We all learn "line upon line, precept upon precept" (2 Nephi 28:30), with the goal being authentic religious faith informing genuine Christlike living. In this there is no place for coercion or manipulation, no place for intimidation or hypocrisy. But no child in this Church should be left with uncertainty about his or her parents' devotion to the Lord Jesus Christ, the Restoration of His Church, and the reality of living prophets and Apostles who, now as in earlier days, lead that Church according to "the will of the Lord, . . . the mind of the Lord, . . . the word of the Lord, . . . and the power of God unto salvation" (D&C 68:4). In such basic matters of faith, prophets do not apologize for requesting unity, indeed conformity, in the eloquent sense that the Prophet Joseph Smith used that latter word (see D&C 128:13). In any case, as Elder Neal Maxwell once said to me in a hallway conversation, "There didn't seem to be any problem with conformity the day the Red Sea opened."

Parents simply cannot flirt with skepticism or cynicism, then be surprised when their children expand that flirtation into full-blown romance. If in matters of faith and belief children are at risk of being swept downstream by this intellectual current or that cultural rapid, we as their parents must be more certain than ever to hold to anchored, unmistakable moorings clearly recognizable to those of our own household. It won't help anyone if we go over the edge with them, explaining through the roar of the falls all the way down that we really did know the Church was true and that the keys of the priesthood really were lodged there but we just didn't want to stifle anyone's freedom to think otherwise. No, we can hardly expect the children to get to shore safely if the parents don't seem to know where to anchor their own boat. Isaiah once used a variation on such imagery when he said of unbelievers, "[Their] tacklings are loosed; they could not . . . strengthen their mast, they could not spread the sail" (Isaiah 33:23).

Parents simply cannot flirt with skepticism or cynicism, then be surprised when their children expand that flirtation into full-blown romance.

I think some parents may not understand that even when they feel secure in their own minds regarding matters of personal testimony, they can nevertheless make that faith too difficult for their children to detect. We can be reasonably active, meeting-going Latter-day Saints, but if we do not live lives of gospel integrity and convey to our children powerful, heartfelt convictions regarding the truthfulness of the Restoration and the divine guidance of the Church from the First Vision to this very hour, then those children may, to our regret but not surprise, turn out *not* to be visibly active, meeting-going Latter-day Saints or sometimes anything close to it.

Sister Holland and I once met a fine young man who came in contact with us after he had been roaming around through the occult and sorting through a variety of Eastern religions, all in an attempt to find religious faith. His father, he admitted, believed in nothing whatsoever. But his grandfather, he said, was actually a member of The Church of Jesus Christ of Latter-day Saints. "But he didn't do much with it," the young man said. "He was always pretty cynical about the Church." From a grandfather who is cynical to a son who is agnostic to a grandson who is now looking desperately for what God had already once given his family! What a classic example of the warning Elder Richard L. Evans once gave:

"Sometimes some parents mistakenly feel that they can relax a little as to conduct and conformity or take perhaps a so called liberal view of basic and fundamental things—thinking that a little laxness or indulgence won't matter—or they may fail to teach or to attend Church, or may voice critical views. Some parents . . . seem to feel that they can ease up a little on the fundamentals without affecting their family or their family's future. *But*," he observed, "*if a parent goes a little off course, the children are likely to exceed the parent's example.*"[1]

To lead a child (or anyone else!), even inadvertently, away from faithfulness, away from loyalty and bedrock belief simply because we want to be clever or independent is license no parent nor any other person has ever been given. In matters of religion a skeptical mind is not a higher manifestation of virtue than is a believing heart. Analytical deconstruction in the field of, say, literary fiction can be just plain old-fashioned destruction when transferred to families yearning for faith at home. And such a deviation from the true course can be deceptively slow and subtle in its impact. As one observer said, if you raise the temperature of my "bath water . . . only 1 degree every 10 minutes, how [will I] know when to scream?"[2]

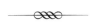

In matters of religion a skeptical mind is not a higher manifestation of virtue than is a believing heart.

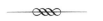

When erecting their sacred tabernacle in the wilderness of Sinai, the ancient children of Israel were commanded to make firm their supporting cords and strengthen the stakes that held them (see Isaiah 54:2; 3 Nephi 22:2). The reason? Storms arise in life—regularly. So fix it, fasten it, then fix and fasten it again. Even then we know that some children will make choices that break their parents' hearts. Moms and dads can do everything right and yet have children who stray. Moral agency still obtains. But even in such painful hours it will be comforting for you to know that your children knew of your abiding faith in Christ, in His true Church, in the keys of the priesthood, and in those who hold them. It will be comforting then for you to know that if your children choose to leave the straight and narrow way, they leave it very conscious that their parents were firmly in it. Furthermore, they will be much more likely to return to that path when they come to themselves (see Luke 15:17) and recall the loving example and gentle teachings you offered them there.

Live the gospel as conspicuously as you can. Keep the covenants your children know you have made. Give priesthood blessings. And bear your testimony![3] Don't just assume your children will somehow get the drift of your beliefs on their own. The prophet Nephi said near the end of his life that his people had written their record of Christ and preserved their convictions regarding His gospel in order "to *persuade* our children . . . that our children may *know* . . . [and believe] the right way" (2 Nephi 25:23, 26, 28; emphasis added).

Nephi-like, might we ask ourselves, what do our children know? From us? Personally? Do our children know that we love the scriptures? Do they see us reading them and marking them and clinging to them in daily life? Have our children ever unexpectedly opened a closed door and found us on our knees in prayer? Have they heard us not only pray *with* them but also pray *for* them out of nothing more than sheer parental love? Do our children know we believe in fasting as something more than an obligatory first-Sunday-of-the-month hardship? Do

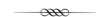

Have our children ever unexpectedly opened a closed door and found us on our knees in prayer?

they know that we have fasted for them and for their future on days about which they knew nothing? Do they know we love being in the temple, not least because it provides a bond to them that neither death nor the legions of hell can break? Do they know we love and sustain local and general leaders, imperfect as they are, for their willingness to accept callings they did not seek in order to preserve a standard of righteousness they did not create? Do those children know that we love God with all our heart and that we long to see the face—and fall at the feet—of His Only Begotten Son? I pray that they know this.

Our children take their flight into the future with our thrust and with our aim. And even as we anxiously watch that arrow in flight and know all the evils that can deflect its course after it has left our hand, nevertheless we take courage in remembering that the most important mortal factor in determining that arrow's destination will be the stability, strength, and unwavering certainty of the holder of the bow.[4]

God will send aid to no one more readily than He will send it to a child—and to the parent of a child.

Carl Sandburg once said, "A baby is God's opinion that life should go on." For that baby's future as well as your own, be strong. Be believing. Keep loving and keep testifying. Keep praying. Those prayers will be heard and answered in the most unexpected hour. God will send aid to no one more readily than He will send it to a child—and to the parent of a child.

"And [Jesus] said unto them: Behold your little ones. And . . . they cast their eyes towards heaven, and they saw the heavens open, and they saw angels descending . . . as it were in the midst of fire; and they came down and encircled those little ones about, and they were encircled about with fire; and the angels did minister unto them" (3 Nephi 17:23–24).

May it always be so, I earnestly pray—for the children.

Notes

From a talk given at general conference, April 2003.

1. In Conference Report, October 1964, 135–36; emphasis added.
2. Marshall McLuhan, quoted in John Leo, "The Proper Place for Commercials," *U.S. News and World Report* (30 October 1989), 71.
3. See Joseph Smith, *Lectures on Faith* (Salt Lake City: Deseret Book, 1985), lecture 2, paragraphs 33–35, for a defining statement on the parental power of human testimony.
4. I am indebted to Kahlil Gibran's *The Prophet* (New York: A. A. Knopf, 1923) for the suggestion of this metaphor.

CHAPTER 3

"Because She Is a Mother"

There are some lines attributed to Victor Hugo that read: "She broke the bread into two fragments and gave them to her children, who ate with eagerness. 'She hath kept none for herself,' grumbled the sergeant.

"'Because she is not hungry,' said a soldier.

"'No,' said the sergeant, 'because she is a mother.'"

In writing to and about mothers I do not neglect the crucial, urgent role of fathers, particularly as fatherlessness in contemporary homes is considered by some to be "the central social problem of our time."[1] Indeed, fatherlessness can be a problem even in a home where the father is present—eating and sleeping, so to speak, "by remote." But that is a priesthood message for another chapter. Here I wish to praise those motherly hands that have rocked the infant's cradle and, through the righteousness taught to their children there, are at the very center of the Lord's purposes for us in mortality.

In so speaking I echo Paul, who wrote in praise of Timothy's "unfeigned faith . . . , which dwelt first," he said, "in thy grandmother Lois, and [in] thy mother Eunice" (2 Timothy 1:5). "From [the days when thou wert] a child," Paul said, "thou hast known the holy scriptures" (2 Timothy 3:15). We give thanks for all the mothers and grandmothers from whom such truths have been learned at such early ages.

In speaking of mothers generally, I especially wish to praise and encourage *young* mothers. The work of a mother is hard, too often unheralded work. The young years are often those when either husband or wife—or both—may still be in school or in those earliest and leanest stages of developing the husband's breadwinning capacities. Finances fluctuate daily between low and nonexistent. The apartment is usually decorated in one of two smart designs: Deseret Industries provincial or early Mother Hubbard. The car, if there is one, runs on smooth tires and an empty tank. But with night feedings and night teethings, often the greatest challenge of all for a young mother is simply fatigue. Through these years, mothers go longer on less sleep and give more to others with less personal renewal for themselves than any other group I know at any other time in life. It is not surprising when the shadows under their eyes sometimes vaguely resemble the state of Rhode Island.

Of course the irony is that this is often the sister we want to call—or need to call—to service in the ward and stake auxiliaries. That's understandable. Who wouldn't want the exemplary influence of these young Loises- and Eunices-in-the-making? It would be well for leaders to be wise, to remember that families are the highest priority of all, especially in those formative years. Even so, young mothers will still find magnificent ways to serve faithfully in the Church, even as others serve and strengthen them—and their families—in like manner.

Do the best you can through these years, but whatever else you do, cherish that role that is so uniquely yours and for which heaven itself sends angels to watch over you and your little ones. Husbands—especially husbands—as well as Church leaders and friends in every direction, be helpful and sensitive and wise. Remember, "To every thing there is a season, and a time to every purpose under the heaven" (Ecclesiastes 3:1).

Whatever else you do, cherish that role that is so uniquely yours and for which heaven itself sends angels to watch over you and your little ones.

Mothers, we acknowledge and esteem your faith in every footstep. Please know that it is worth it then, now, and forever. And if, for whatever reason, you are making this courageous effort alone, without your husband at your side, then our prayers will be all the greater for you, and our determination to lend a helping hand even more resolute.

One young mother wrote to me recently that her anxiety tended to come on three fronts. One was that whenever she heard talks on LDS motherhood, she worried because she felt she didn't measure up or somehow wasn't going to be equal to the task. Second, she felt like the world expected her to teach her children reading, writing, interior design, Latin, calculus, and the Internet—all before the baby said something terribly ordinary, like "goo goo." Third, she felt people were sometimes patronizing, almost always without meaning to be, because the advice she got or even the compliments she received seemed to reflect nothing of the mental investment, the spiritual and emotional exertion, the long-night, long-day, stretched-to-the-limit demands that sometimes were required in her trying to be and wanting to be the mother God hopes she will be.

But one thing, she said, keeps her going: "Through the thick and the thin of this, and through the occasional tears of it all, *I know deep down inside I am doing God's work.* I know that in my motherhood I am in an eternal partnership with Him. I am deeply moved that God finds His ultimate purpose and meaning in being a parent, even if some of His children make Him weep.

"It is this realization," she says, "that I try to recall on those inevitably difficult days when all of this can be a bit overwhelming. Maybe it is precisely our inability and anxiousness that urge us to reach out to Him and enhance His ability to reach back to us. Maybe He secretly hopes we *will* be anxious," she said, "and *will* plead for His help. Then, I believe, He can teach these children directly, through us, but with no resistance offered. I like that idea," she concludes. "It gives me hope. If I can be right before my Father in Heaven, perhaps His guidance to our children can be unimpeded. Maybe then it can be *His* work and *His* glory in a very literal sense."

In light of that kind of expression, it is clear that some of those Rhode Island-sized shadows come not just from diapers and carpooling but from at least a few sleepless nights spent searching the soul, seeking earnestly for the capacity to raise these children to be what God wants them to be. Moved by that kind of devotion and determination, may I say to mothers collectively, in the name of the Lord, you are magnificent. You are doing terrifically well. The very fact that you have been given such a responsibility is everlasting evidence of the trust your Father in Heaven has in you. He knows that your giving birth to a child does not immediately propel you into the circle of the omniscient. If you and your husband will strive to love God and live the gospel yourselves; if you will plead for that guidance and comfort of the Holy Spirit promised to the faithful; if you will go to the temple to both make and claim the promises of the most sacred covenants a woman or man can make in this world; if you will show others, including your children, the same caring, compassionate, forgiving heart you want heaven to show you; if you try your best to be the best parent you can be, you will have done all that a human being can do and all that God expects you to do.

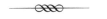

If you try your best to be the best parent you can be, you will have done all that a human being can do and all that God expects you to do.

Sometimes the decision of a child or a grandchild will break your heart. Sometimes expectations won't immediately be met. Every mother and father worries about that. Even that beloved and wonderfully successful parent President Joseph F. Smith pled, "Oh! God, let me not lose my own."[2] That is every parent's cry, and in it is something of every parent's fear. But no one has failed who keeps trying and keeps praying. You have every right to receive encouragement and to know in the end your children will call your name blessed, just like those generations of foremothers before you who hoped your same hopes and felt your same fears.

Yours is the grand tradition of Eve, the mother of all the human family, the one who understood that she and Adam *had* to fall in order that "men [and women] might be" and that there would be joy (2 Nephi 2:25). Yours is the grand tradition of Sarah and Rebekah and Rachel, without whom there could not have been those magnificent patriarchal promises to Abraham, Isaac, and Jacob that bless us all. Yours is the grand tradition of Lois and Eunice and the mothers of the 2,000 stripling warriors.

Yours is the grand tradition of Mary, chosen and foreordained from before this world was, to conceive, carry, and bear the Son of God Himself. We thank all of you, including our own mothers, and tell you there is nothing more important in this world than participating so directly in the work and glory of God, in bringing to pass the mortality and earthly life of His daughters and sons, so that immortality and eternal life can come in those celestial realms on high.

Yours is the work of salvation, and therefore you will be magnified, compensated, made more than you are and better than you have ever been as you try to make honest effort, however feeble you may sometimes feel that to be.

When you have come to the Lord in meekness and lowliness of heart and, as one mother said, "pounded on the doors of heaven to ask for, to plead for, to demand guidance and wisdom and help for this wondrous task," that door is thrown open to provide you the influence and the help of all eternity. Claim the promises of the Savior of the world. Ask for the healing balm of the Atonement for whatever may be troubling you or your children. Know that in faith things will be made right in spite of you, or more correctly, because of you.

You can't possibly do this alone, but you *do* have help. The Master of heaven and earth is there to bless you—He who resolutely goes after the lost sheep, sweeps thoroughly to find the lost coin, waits everlastingly for the return of the prodigal son. Yours is the work of salvation, and therefore you will be magnified, compensated, made more than you are and better than you have ever been as you try to make honest effort, however feeble you may sometimes feel that to be.

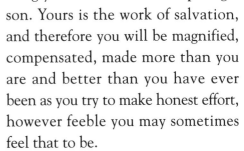

You are doing God's work. You are doing it wonderfully well. He is blessing you and He will bless you, even—no, especially—when your days and your nights may be the most challenging.

Remember, remember all the days of your motherhood: "ye have not come thus far save it were by the word of Christ with unshaken faith in him, relying wholly upon the merits of him who is mighty to save" (2 Nephi 31:19).

Rely on Him. Rely on Him heavily. Rely on Him forever. And "press forward with a steadfastness in Christ, having a perfect brightness of hope" (2 Nephi 31:20). You are doing God's work. You are doing it wonderfully well. He is blessing you and He will bless you, even—no, *especially*—when your days and your nights may be the most challenging. Like the woman who anonymously, meekly, perhaps even with hesitation and some embarrassment, fought her way through the crowd just to touch the hem of the Master's garment, so Christ will say to the women who worry and wonder and sometimes weep over their responsibility as mothers, "Daughter, be of good comfort; thy faith hath made thee whole" (Matthew 9:22). And faith—yours and your children's—will make your children whole as well.

NOTES

From a talk given at general conference, April 1997.

1. Tom Lowe, "Fatherlessness: The Central Social Problem of Our Time," Claremont Institute Home Page Editorial, January 1996.
2. Joseph F. Smith, *Gospel Doctrine*, 5th ed. (Salt Lake City: Deseret Book, 1939), 462.

CHAPTER 4

THE HANDS OF THE FATHERS

In considering the beauty and power of the Atonement, I find myself feeling gratitude not only for the resurrected Lord Jesus Christ but also for His true Father, our spiritual Father and God, who, by accepting the sacrifice of His firstborn, perfect Son, blessed all of His children in those hours of redemption. There is so much meaning in the declaration from John the Beloved that praises the Father as well as the Son: "For God so loved the world, that he gave his only begotten Son, that whosoever believeth in him should not perish, but have everlasting life" (John 3:16).

I am a father, inadequate to be sure, but I cannot comprehend the burden it must have been for God in His heaven to witness the deep suffering and crucifixion of His Beloved Son in such a manner. His every impulse and instinct *must* have been to stop it, to send angels to intervene—but He did not intervene. He endured what He saw because it was the only way that a saving, vicarious payment could be made for the sins of all His other children from Adam and Eve to the end of the world. I am eternally grateful for a perfect Father and His perfect Son, neither of whom shrank from the bitter cup nor forsook the rest of us who are imperfect, who fall short and stumble, who too often miss the mark.

This relationship between Christ and His Father is one of the sweetest and most moving themes running through the Savior's ministry. Jesus' entire being, His complete purpose and delight, were centered in pleasing His Father and obeying His will. Of Him He seemed always to be thinking; to Him He seemed always to be praying. Unlike us, He needed no crisis, no discouraging shift in events to direct His hopes heavenward. He was already instinctively, longingly looking that way.

In all His mortal ministry Christ seems never to have had a single moment of vanity or self-interest. When one young man tried to call Him "good," He deflected the compliment, saying only one was deserving of such praise: His Father (see Matthew 19:17).

Jesus' entire being, His complete purpose and delight, were centered in pleasing His Father and obeying His will.

In the early days of His ministry He said humbly, "I can of mine own self do nothing: . . . I seek not mine own will, but the will of the Father which hath sent me" (John 5:30).

Following His teachings, which stunned the audience with their power and authority, He would say: "My doctrine is not mine, but his that sent me. . . . I am not come of myself, but he that sent me is true" (John 7:16, 28). Later he would say again,

"I have not spoken of myself; but the Father which sent me, he gave me a commandment, what I should say, and what I should speak" (John 12:49).

To those who wanted to see the Father, to hear from God directly that Jesus was what He said He was, He answered, "If ye had known me, ye should have known my Father also: . . . he that hath seen me hath seen the Father" (John 14:7, 9). When Jesus wanted to preserve unity among His disciples, He prayed using the example of His own relationship with God: "Holy Father, keep through thine own name those whom thou hast given me, that they may be one, as we are [one]" (John 17:11).

Even as He moved toward the Crucifixion, He restrained His Apostles who would have intervened by saying, "The cup which my Father hath given me, shall I not drink it?" (John 18:11). When that unspeakable ordeal was finished, He uttered what must have been the most peaceful and deserved words of His mortal ministry. At the end of His agony, He whispered, "It is finished. . . . Father, into thy hands I commend my spirit" (John 19:30; Luke 23:46). Finally it was over. Finally He could go home.

I confess that I have reflected at length upon that moment and the Resurrection that was shortly to follow it. I have wondered what that reunion must have been like: the Father who loved this Son so much, the Son who honored and revered His Father in every word and deed. For two who were one as these two were one, what must that embrace have been like? What must that divine companionship be yet? We can only wonder and admire. And we can yearn to live worthily of some portion of that relationship ourselves.

As a father, I wonder if I and all other fathers could do more to build a sweeter, stronger relationship with our sons and daughters here on earth. Dads, is it too bold to hope that our children might have some small portion of the feeling for us that the Divine Son felt for His Father? Might we earn more of that love by trying to be more of what God was to His child? In any case, we do know that a young person's developing concept of God centers on characteristics observed in that child's earthly parents.[1]

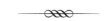

Is it too bold to hope that our children might have some small portion of the feeling for us that the Divine Son felt for His Father?

For that reason and many others, I suppose no book I have read in recent months has alarmed me more than a work entitled *Fatherless America*. In this study the author speaks of "fatherlessness" as "the most harmful demographic trend of this generation," the leading cause of damage to children. It is, he is convinced, the engine driving our most urgent social problems, from poverty to crime to adolescent pregnancy to child abuse to domestic violence. Among the principal social issues of our time is the flight of fathers from their children's lives.[2]

Of even greater concern than the physical absenteeism of some fathers is the spiritually or emotionally absent father. These are fatherly sins of omission that are probably more destructive than sins of commission. Why are we not surprised that when 2,000 children of all ages and backgrounds were asked what they appreciated most about their fathers, they answered universally, "He spends time with me"?[3]

A young Laurel I met on a conference assignment wrote to me after our visit: "I wish my dad knew how much I need him spiritually and emotionally. I crave any kind comment, any warm personal gesture. I don't think he knows how much it would mean to me to have him take an active interest in what is going on in my life, to offer to give me a blessing, or just spend some time together. I know he worries that he won't do the right thing or won't say the words well. But just to have him *try* would mean more than he could ever know. I don't want to sound ungrateful because I know he loves me. He sent me a note once and signed it 'Love, Dad.' I treasure that note. I hold it among my dearest possessions."

Well, as with that young woman, I don't want to seem ungrateful or to make fathers feel they have fallen short. Most fathers are wonderful. Most dads are terrific. As Edgar A. Guest wrote in these little storybook verses remembered from my youth:

> *Only a dad with a tired face,*
> *Coming home from the daily race . . .*
> *Glad in his heart that his own rejoice*
> *To see him come home and to hear his voice. . . .*
>
> *Only a dad, neither rich nor proud,*
> *Merely one of the surging crowd,*
> *Toiling, striving from day to day,*
> *Facing whatever may come his way, . . .*
>
> *Only a dad but he gives his all,*
> *To smooth the way for his children small,*
> *Doing with courage stern and grim*
> *The deeds that his father did for him.*
> *This is the line that for him I pen,*
> *Only a dad, but the best of men.*[4]

And even when we are *not* "the best of men," even in our limitations and inadequacy, we can keep making our way in the right direction because of the encouraging teachings set forth by a Divine Father and demonstrated by a Divine Son. With a Heavenly Father's help we can leave more of a parental legacy than we suppose.

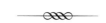

With a Heavenly Father's help we can leave more of a parental legacy than we suppose.

One new father wrote to me: "Often as I watch my son watch me, I am taken back to moments with my own dad, remembering how vividly I wanted to be just like him. I remember having a plastic razor and my own can of foaming cream, and each morning I would shave when he shaved. I remember following his footsteps back and forth across the grass as he mowed the lawn in summer.

"Now I want my son to follow my lead, and yet it terrifies me to know he probably will. Holding this little boy in my arms, I feel a 'heavenly homesickness,' a longing to love the way God loves, to comfort the way He comforts, to protect the way He protects. The answer to all the fears of my youth was always 'What would Dad do?' Now that I have a child to raise I am counting on a Heavenly Father to tell me exactly that."

And a friend from college days wrote to me: "Much in my chaotic childhood was uncertain, but one thing I knew for sure: that my dad loved me. That certainty was the anchor of my young life. I came to know and love the Lord because my father loved him. I have never called anyone a fool or taken the Lord's name in vain because he told me the Bible said I shouldn't. I have always paid my tithing because he taught me it was a privilege to do so. I have always tried to take responsibility for my mistakes because my father did. Even though he was estranged from the Church for a [time], at the end of his life he served a mission and worked faithfully in the temple. In his will he said that any money left over from taking care of his [family] should go to the Church. He loved the Church with all of his heart. And because of him, so do I."

Surely that must be the spiritual application of Lord Byron's couplet from his poem "Parisina": "Yet in my lineaments they trace / Some features of my father's face."

At a vulnerable moment in young Nephi's life, his prophetic future was determined when he said, "I did believe all the words which had been spoken by my father" (1 Nephi 2:16). At the turning point of the prophet Enos' life, he said it was "the words which I had often heard my father speak" (Enos 1:3) that prompted one of the great revelations recorded in the Book of Mormon. And sorrowing Alma the Younger, when confronted by the excruciating memory of his sins, "remembered also to have heard [his] father prophesy . . . concerning the coming of . . . Jesus Christ, a Son of God, to atone for the sins of the world" (Alma 36:17). That brief memory, that personal testimony offered by his father at a time when the father may have felt that nothing was sinking in, not only saved the spiritual life of this, his son, but changed forever the history of the Book of Mormon people.

Of Abraham, the grand patriarch, God said, "*I know him*, . . . he will command his children and his household after him, and they shall keep the way of the Lord" (Genesis 18:19; emphasis added).

I bear my witness that "great things [will] be required at the hand[s] of [the] fathers," as the Lord declared to the Prophet

Joseph Smith (D&C 29:48). Surely the greatest of those things will be to have done all they could for the happiness and spiritual safety of the children they are to nurture.

In that most burdensome moment of all human history, with blood appearing at every pore and an anguished cry upon His lips, Christ sought Him whom He had always sought—His Father. "Abba," he cried, "Papa," or from the lips of a younger child, something akin to "Daddy" (Mark 14:36).

This is such a personal moment it almost seems a sacrilege to cite it. A Son in unrelieved pain, a Father His only true source of strength, both of them staying the course, making it through the night—together.

Fathers, may we be renewed in our task as parents, bolstered by images of this Father and this Son as we embrace our children and stand with them forever.

NOTES

From a talk given at general conference, April 1999.

1. See "Parent-Child Relationships and Children's Images of God," *Journal for the Scientific Study of Religion,* March 1997, 25–43.
2. David Blankenhorn, *Fatherless America: Confronting Our Most Urgent Social Problem* (Basic Books, 1995), 1.
3. See "Becoming a Better Father," *Ensign,* January 1983, 27.
4. Edgar A. Guest, "Only a Dad," in *A Heap o' Livin'* (Chicago: Reilly & Lee, 1916), 42.

CHAPTER 5

To Young Women

Father Time played a rude trick on me not long ago. I arose one morning all bright eyed and bushy tailed, greeted the dawn with a smile—only to realize suddenly that with the birthday to be celebrated that day I now had a teenage grandchild. I thought about it for a minute and then did what any responsible, dignified adult would do. I got back in bed and pulled the covers over my head.

Traditional joking aside about the harrowing experience of raising teenagers, I want to express to my own granddaughter and the vast majority of the youth of the Church whom I meet around the world how extraordinarily proud we are of them. Moral and physical danger exists almost everywhere around them and temptations of a dozen kinds present themselves daily, yet most of them strive to do what is right.

Because this precious eldest grandchild of whom I spoke is a young woman, I am going to address this chapter to the young women of the Church, but I hope the spirit of what I write can apply to women and men of all ages. Here, however, as Maurice Chevalier used to sing, I want to "thank heaven for little girls."

First of all, I want you to be proud you are a woman. I want you to feel the reality of what that means, to know who you truly are. You are literally a spirit daughter of heavenly parents with a divine nature and an eternal destiny.[1] That surpassing truth should be fixed deep in your soul and be fundamental to every decision you make as you grow into mature womanhood. There could never be a greater authentication of your dignity, your worth, your privileges, and your promise. Your Father in Heaven knows your name and knows your circumstance. He hears your prayers. He knows your hopes and dreams, including your fears and frustrations. And He knows what you can become through faith in Him.

Because of this divine heritage, you, along with all of your spiritual sisters and brothers, have full equality in His sight and are empowered through obedience to become a rightful heir in His eternal kingdom, an heir of God, and joint-heir with Christ (see Romans 8:17). Seek to comprehend the significance of these doctrines. Everything Christ taught He taught to women as well as men. Indeed, in the restored light of the gospel of Jesus Christ, a woman, including a young woman, occupies a majesty all her own in the divine design of the

Your Father in Heaven knows your name and knows your circumstance. He hears your prayers. He knows your hopes and dreams, including your fears and frustrations.

Creator. You are, as Elder James E. Talmage once phrased it, "a sanctified investiture which none shall dare profane."[2]

Be a woman of Christ. Cherish your esteemed place in the sight of God. He needs you. This Church needs you. The world needs you. A woman's abiding trust in God and unfailing devotion to things of the Spirit have always been an anchor when the wind and the waves of life were fiercest.[3] I say to you what the Prophet Joseph said more than 150 years ago: "If you live up to your privileges, the angels cannot be restrained from being your associates."[4]

All of this is to try to tell you how your Father in Heaven feels about you and what He has designed for you to become. And if for a time you are less visionary than this or seem bent on living beneath your privilege, then we express even greater love for you and plead with you to make your teenage years a triumph, not a tragedy. Fathers and mothers, prophets and Apostles have no motive except to bless your life and to spare you every possible heartache we can spare you.

For you to fully claim Heavenly Father's blessings and protection, we ask you to stay true to the standards of the gospel of Jesus Christ and *not* slavishly follow the whims of fads and fashions. The Church will never deny your moral agency regarding what you should wear and how you should look. But the Church will always declare standards and will always teach principles. One of those principles is modesty. In

In the gospel of Jesus Christ, modesty in appearance is always *in fashion. Our standards are not socially negotiable.*

the gospel of Jesus Christ, modesty in appearance is *always* in fashion. Our standards are not socially negotiable.

The *For the Strength of Youth* pamphlet is very clear in its call for young women to avoid clothing that is too tight, too short, or improperly revealing in any manner, including bare midriffs.[5] Choose your clothing the way you would choose your friends— in both cases choose that which improves you and would give you confidence standing in the presence of God (see D&C 121:45). Good friends would never embarrass you, demean you, or exploit you. Neither should your clothing.

I make a special appeal regarding how young women might dress for Church services and Sabbath worship. We used to speak of "best dress" or "Sunday dress," and maybe we should do so again. In any case, from ancient times to modern we have always been invited to present our best selves inside and out when entering the house of the Lord—and a dedicated LDS chapel is a "house of the Lord." Our clothing or footwear need never be expensive, indeed should *not* be expensive, but neither should it appear that we are on our way to the beach. When we come to worship the God and Father of us all and to partake of the sacrament symbolizing the Atonement of Jesus Christ, we should be as comely and respectful, as dignified and appropriate as we can be. We should be recognizable in appearance as well as in behavior that we truly are disciples of Christ, that in a spirit of worship we are meek and lowly of

We should be recognizable in appearance as well as in behavior that we truly are disciples of Christ.

heart, that we truly desire the Savior's Spirit to be with us always.

In this same vein may I address an even more sensitive subject. I plead with you to please be more accepting of yourself, including your body shape and style, with a little less longing to look like someone else. We are all different. Some are tall, and some are short. Some are round, and some are thin. And almost everyone at some time or other wants to be something he or she is not! But as one adviser to teenage girls said: "You can't live your life worrying that the world is staring at you. When you let people's opinions make you self-conscious you give away your power. . . . The key to feeling [confident] is to always listen to your inner self—[the *real* you.]"[6] And in the kingdom of God, the real you is "more precious than rubies" (Proverbs 3:15). Every young woman is a child of destiny and every adult woman a powerful force for good. I mention adult women because they are our greatest examples and resource for these young women. And if a woman is obsessing over being a size 2, she won't be very surprised when her daughter or the Mia Maid in her class does the same and makes herself physically ill trying to accomplish it. We should all be as fit as we can be—that's good Word of Wisdom doctrine. That means eating right and exercising and helping our bodies function at their optimum strength. We could probably all do better in that regard. But I speak here of optimum health; there is no universal optimum size.

Frankly, the world has been brutal with you in this regard. You are bombarded in movies, television, fashion magazines, and advertisements with the message that looks are everything! The pitch is, "If your looks are good enough, your life will be glamorous and you will be happy and popular." That kind of pressure is immense in the teenage years, to say nothing of later womanhood. In too many cases too much is being done to the human body to meet just such a fictional (to say nothing of superficial) standard.

In terms of preoccupation with self and a fixation on the physical, this is more than social insanity; it is spiritually destructive, and it accounts for much of the unhappiness women, including young women, face in the modern world. And if adults are preoccupied with appearance—tucking and nipping and implanting and remodeling everything that can be remodeled—those pressures and anxieties will certainly seep through to children. At some point the problem becomes what the Book of Mormon called "vain imaginations" (1 Nephi 12:18). And in secular society both vanity *and* imagination run wild. One would truly need a great and spacious makeup kit to compete with beauty as portrayed in media all around us. Yet at the end of the day there would still be those "in the attitude of mocking and pointing their fingers" as Lehi saw (1 Nephi 8:27), because however much one tries in the world of glamour and fashion, it will never be glamorous enough.

One would truly need a great and spacious makeup kit to compete with beauty as portrayed in media all around us.

A woman not of our faith once wrote something to the effect that in her years of working with beautiful women she had seen several things they all had in common, and not one of them had anything to do with sizes and shapes. She said the loveliest women she had known had a glow of health, a warm personality, a love of learning, stability of character, and integrity. If we may add the sweet and gentle Spirit of the Lord carried by such a woman, then this describes the loveliness of women in any age or time, *every* element of which is emphasized in and attainable through the blessings of the gospel of Jesus Christ.

Much has been said lately in entertainment media about the current craze for "reality shows." I am not sure what those are, but from the bottom of my heart I share this gospel reality with the beautiful generation of young women growing up in this Church.

My solemn declaration to you is that the Father and the Son did *in very fact* appear to the Prophet Joseph Smith, himself a young man called by God from your very age group. I testify that these divine beings spoke to him, that he heard their eternal voices, and he saw their glorified bodies (see Joseph Smith—History 1:24–25). That experience was as real in its own setting as the Apostle Thomas's was when the Savior said to him, "Reach hither thy finger, and behold my hands; and reach hither thy hand, and thrust it into my side: . . . be not faithless, but [be] believing" (John 20:27).

To my granddaughter and to every other young person in this Church I bear my personal witness that God is *in reality* our Father and Jesus Christ is *in reality* His Only Begotten Son in the flesh, the Savior and Redeemer of the world. I testify that this *really* is the Church and kingdom of God on earth, that true prophets have led this people in the past and a true prophet leads it now. As you come to know the unending love the leaders of the Church have for you, the eternal realities of the gospel of Jesus Christ will lift you above temporal concerns and teenage anxieties.

NOTES

From a talk given at general conference, October 2005.

1. See "The Family: A Proclamation to the World," *Ensign*, November 1995, 102.
2. James E. Talmage, "The Eternity of Sex," *Young Woman's Journal*, October 1914, 602.
3. See J. Reuben Clark in Conference Report, April 1940, 21, for a lengthy tribute to women of the Church.
4. Joseph Smith, *History of The Church of Jesus Christ of Latter-day Saints*, 7 vols. (Salt Lake City: The Church of Jesus Christ of Latter-day Saints, 1932–1952), 4:605.
5. *For the Strength of Youth*, pamphlet (Salt Lake City: The Church of Jesus Christ of Latter-day Saints, 2001), 15.
6. Julia DeVillers, *Teen People*, September 2005, 104.

CHAPTER 6

"LET VIRTUE GARNISH THY THOUGHTS UNCEASINGLY"

⸺⚬⚭⚬⸺

An article I read recently said the most common illness among young people today is not diabetes or heart disease or cancer. (Those kinds of problems are usually reserved for people *my* age.) No, the illness that those in their teens and twenties suffer from most, it was reported, is self-doubt, fear about the future, low self-esteem, and a general lack of confidence in themselves and in the world around them.

There are plenty of troubles in the world, but there have always been troubles in every age and era. Don't be preoccupied with them and don't be discouraged by them. Our time is filled with wonderful opportunities and great blessings. We will continue to have advances in science and technology, medicine and communication—all the fields that do so much to enrich our lives. We live in the most glorious age the world has ever known, with more of the blessings of the day coming to more people around the world than at any other time in history. Remember—your grandmother never dreamed of an iPod when she was a teenager, and your grandfather still has no idea how to text message. So, be happy and healthy and optimistic.

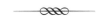

Still, I do understand the kinds of concerns you feel, because for most of my young life I, too, seemed to face situations in which I didn't have very much self-confidence. I can remember striving for good grades, hoping to win a chance for a scholarship, and wondering why others seemed more gifted in that category than I. I can remember years and

Your grandmother never dreamed of an iPod when she was a teenager, and your grandfather still has no idea how to text message.

years of athletic contests in which I tried to play with the confidence necessary for success in high school and college sports, wanting so desperately to win the big game or bring home a coveted championship. I especially remember lacking confidence with girls, so often the great anxiety producer in young men. I am so grateful Sister Holland took a chance on me. Yes, I can remember all the things you remember—not being sure about how I looked or if I was accepted or what the future would hold for me.

We are not in a position to discuss here all those issues a young person faces that bring some self-doubt and some lack of confidence, but I wish to speak pointedly about how to have a very special kind of confidence. This confidence, when rightfully earned, does wonders for every other aspect of our lives, especially our self-esteem and how we view the future. To make this point I need to tell a story.

Many years ago now, long before I was called as a General Authority, I participated as a speaker in a Young Adult conference in a distant state. The conference concluded with a testimony meeting in which a handsome young returned missionary stood up to bear his testimony. He looked good—clean and confident—just like a returned missionary should look.

As he began to speak, tears came to his eyes. He said he was grateful to stand in the midst of such a terrific group of young Latter-day Saints and to feel good about the life he was trying to lead. But that feeling had only been possible, he said, because of an experience he had had a few years earlier, an experience that had shaped his life forever.

He then told of coming home from a date shortly after he had been ordained an elder at age eighteen. Something had happened on this date of which he was not proud. He did not go into any details, nor should he have done so in a public setting. To this day I do not know the nature of the incident, but it was significant enough to him to have affected his spirit and his self-esteem.

As he sat in his car for a while in the driveway of his own home, thinking things through and feeling genuine sorrow for whatever had happened, his nonmember mother came running frantically from the house straight to his car. In an instant she conveyed that this boy's younger brother—I do not know what the age of the younger boy was—had just fallen in the home, had hit his head sharply, and was having some kind of seizure or convulsion. The nonmember father had immediately called 911, but it would take some time at best for help to come.

"Come and do something," she cried. "Isn't there something

you do in your Church at times like this? You have their priesthood. Come and do something." His mother didn't know a lot about the Church at that point, but she knew something of priesthood blessings.

Nevertheless, on this night when someone he loved dearly needed his faith and his strength, this young man could not respond. Given the feelings he had just been wrestling with, and the compromise he felt he had just made—whatever that was—he could not bring himself to go before the Lord and ask for the blessing that was needed.

He bolted from the car and ran down the street several hundred yards to the home of a worthy older man who had befriended him in the ward ever since the boy's conversion two or three years earlier. An explanation was given, the older man responded, and the two were back at the house still well before the paramedics got there. The happy ending of this story as told in that testimony meeting was that this older man instantly gave a sweet, powerful priesthood blessing, leaving the injured child stable and resting by the time medical help arrived. A quick trip to the hospital and a thorough exam there revealed that no permanent damage had been done. A very fearful moment for this family had passed.

Then the returned missionary of whom I speak said this: "No one who has not faced what I faced that night will ever know the shame I felt and the sorrow I bore for not feeling worthy to use my priesthood. It is an even more painful memory for me because it was my own little brother who needed me, and my beloved nonmember parents who were so fearful and who had a right to expect more of me. But as I stand before you today I can promise you this," he said. "I am not perfect, but from that night onward I have never done anything that would keep me from going before the Lord with confidence and asking for His help when it is needed. Personal worthiness is a battle in this world in which we live," he acknowledged, "but it is a battle I am winning. I have felt the finger of condemnation pointing at me once in my life, and I don't intend to feel it ever again if I can do anything about it. And, of course," he concluded, "I can do *everything* about it."

To have the approval of your conscience when you are alone with your memories can allow you to feel the Spirit of God in a very personal way.

He finished his testimony and sat down. I can still picture him. I can still see the setting we were in. And I can still remember the stark, moving silence that followed his remarks as everyone in the room had occasion to search his or her soul a little deeper, vowing a little stronger to live by these powerful words given by the Lord: "Let virtue garnish thy thoughts unceasingly; *then shall thy confidence wax strong in the presence of God;* and the doctrine of the priesthood shall distil upon thy soul as the dews from heaven. The Holy Ghost shall be thy constant companion, and thy scepter an unchanging scepter of righteousness and truth" (D&C 121:45–46; emphasis added).

Despite any trials and concerns you have, I want you to think the best and hope the best and have faith in the future. You have a great life ahead of you. Your Heavenly Father loves you. If any mistakes have been made, they can be repented of and forgiven just as they were for this young man. You have everything to live for and plan for and believe in. To have the approval of your conscience when you are alone with your memories can allow you to feel the Spirit of God in a very personal way. I want you to enjoy that Spirit, to feel that confidence in the presence of the Lord always.

NOTE

From a New Year's Eve fireside address, given December 31, 2006.

THE POWER OF THE WORD

CHAPTER 7

"A TEACHER COME FROM GOD"

When Nicodemus came to Jesus early in the Savior's ministry, he spoke for all of us when he said, "Rabbi, we know that thou art a teacher come from God" (John 3:2).

Christ was, of course, much more than a teacher. He was the very Son of God, the Holy One of the eternal gospel plan, the Savior and Redeemer of the world.

But Nicodemus was starting about the way you and I started, the way any child or young student or new convert begins—by recognizing and responding to a thrilling teacher who touches the innermost feelings of our heart.

President Gordon B. Hinckley often called on us to hold our people close to the Church, especially the newly converted member. In issuing this call, he reminded us that we all need at least three things to remain firmly in the faith: a friend, a

57

responsibility, and "[nourishing] by the good word of God" (Moroni 6:4).[1]

Inspired instruction in the home and in the Church helps provide this crucial element of nourishing by the good word of God. To teach effectively and to feel you are succeeding is demanding work indeed. But it is worth it. We can receive "no greater call."[2] Surely the opportunity to magnify that call exists everywhere. The need for it is everlasting. Fathers, mothers, siblings, friends, missionaries, home and visiting teachers, priesthood and auxiliary leaders, classroom instructors—each is, in his or her own way, "come from God" for our schooling and our salvation. In this Church it is virtually impossible to find anyone who is *not* a guide of one kind or another to his or her fellow members of the flock. Little wonder that Paul would say in his writings, "God hath set some in the church, first apostles, secondarily prophets, thirdly teachers" (1 Corinthians 12:28).

For each of us to "come unto Christ" (D&C 20:59), to keep His commandments, and to follow His example back to the Father is surely the highest and holiest purpose of human existence. To help others do that as well—to teach, persuade, and prayerfully lead them to walk that path of redemption also— surely that must be the second most significant task in our lives. Perhaps that is why President David O. McKay once said, "No greater responsibility can rest upon any man [or woman] than to be a teacher of God's children."[3]

We are, in fact, all somewhat like the man of Ethiopia to whom Philip was sent. Like him, we may know enough to reach out for religion. We may invest ourselves in the scriptures. We may even give up our earthly treasures, but without sufficient instruction we may miss the meaning of all this and the requirements that still lie before us. So we cry with this man of great authority, "How can [we understand], except some [teacher] should guide [us]?" (Acts 8:31).

The Apostle Paul taught: "For whosoever shall call upon the name of the Lord shall be saved. [But] how then shall they call on him in whom they have not believed? and how shall they believe in him of whom they have not heard? . . . *Faith cometh by hearing,* and hearing by the word of God" (Romans 10:13–14, 17; emphasis added).

Now, at a time when people everywhere need more faith through hearing the word of God, we must revitalize and reenthrone superior teaching in the Church—at home, from the pulpit, in our administrative meetings, and surely in the classroom. Inspired teaching must never become a lost art in the Church, and we must make certain our quest for it does not become a lost tradition.

President Spencer W. Kimball once pled: "Stake presidents, bishops, and branch presidents, please take a particular interest in improving the quality of teaching in the Church. . . . I fear," he said, "that all too often many of our members come to church, sit through a class or a meeting, and . . . then return home having been largely [uninspired]. It is espe-

Now, at a time when people everywhere need more faith through hearing the word of God, we must revitalize and reenthrone superior teaching in the Church.

cially unfortunate when this happens at a time . . . of stress, temptation, or crisis [in their life]. We all need to be touched and nurtured by the Spirit," he said, "and *effective teaching* is one of the most important ways this can happen. We often do vigorous work," President Kimball concluded, "to get members to come to Church but then do not adequately watch over what they receive when they do come."[4]

On this subject President Gordon B. Hinckley said: "Effective teaching is the very essence of leadership in the Church." May I repeat that. *"Effective teaching is the very essence of leadership in the Church.* Eternal life," President Hinckley continued, "will come only as men and women are taught with such effectiveness that they change and discipline their lives. They cannot be coerced into righteousness or into heaven. They must be led, and that means teaching."[5]

Among the last words the Savior said to His disciples and among the first words He says to us today are: "Go ye therefore, and teach all nations. . . . [Teach] them to observe all things whatsoever I have commanded you: and, lo, I am with you alway, even unto the end of the world" (Matthew 28:19–20). To Peter, the apostolic leader of the Church, the resurrected and ascending Christ said, "Feed my lambs. . . . Feed my sheep. . . . Follow [thou] me" (John 21:15–19).

In all of this we must remember that the Lord has never given more emphatic counsel to the Church than that we are to teach the gospel "by the Spirit, even the Comforter which was sent forth to teach the truth." Do we teach the gospel "by the Spirit of truth?" He has inquired. Or do we teach it "some other way? And if it be by some other way," He warns, "it is not of God" (D&C 50:17–18). In language echoing other commandments, He has said, "If ye receive not the Spirit ye shall not teach" (D&C 42:14).

No eternal learning can take place without that quickening of the Spirit from heaven. So, as parents, teachers, and leaders, we must face our tasks the way Moses faced the promised land.

Knowing he could not succeed any other way, Moses said to Jehovah, "If thy presence go not with me, carry us not up hence" (Exodus 33:15).

That is what our members really want when they gather in a meeting or come into a classroom anyway. Most people don't come to church looking merely for a few new gospel facts or to see old friends, though all of that is important. They come seeking a spiritual experience. They want peace. They want their faith fortified and their hope renewed. They want, in short, to be nourished by the good word of God, to be strengthened by the powers of heaven. Those of us who are called upon to speak or teach or lead have an obligation to help provide that, the best we possibly can. We can only do that if we ourselves are striving to know God, if we ourselves are continually seeking the light of His Only Begotten Son. Then, if our hearts are right, if we are as clean as we can be, if we have prayed and wept and prepared and worried until we don't know what more we can do, God can say to us as He did to Alma and the sons of Mosiah: "Lift up thy head and rejoice. . . . I will give unto you success" (Alma 8:15; 26:27).

Most people don't come to church looking merely for a few new gospel facts or to see old friends, though all of that is important. They come seeking a spiritual experience.

We do have a legitimate worry about the new member, wanting each one to stay with us and enjoy the full blessings of the Church. I am just simple enough to think that if we continue to *teach them*—with the same Christlike spirit, conviction, doctrine, and personal interest the missionaries have shown

them—new converts will not only stay with us but, quite literally, could not be kept away.

The need for continuing such solid teaching is obvious. In
times like ours we *all* need what Mormon called "the virtue of
the word of God" because, he said, it "had [a] more powerful
effect upon the minds of the people
than the sword, or anything else,
which had happened unto them"
(Alma 31:5). When crises come in
our lives—and they will—the
philosophies of men interlaced with a
few scriptures and poems just won't
do. Are we really nurturing our youth
and our new members in a way that
will sustain them when the stresses of
life appear? Or are we giving them
a kind of theological Twinkie—
spiritually empty calories? President
John Taylor once called such teach-
ing "fried froth," the kind of thing you could eat all day and yet
finish feeling totally unsatisfied.[6] During a severe winter several
years ago, President Boyd K. Packer noted that a goodly number of deer had died of starvation while their stomachs were full
of hay. In an honest effort to assist, agencies had supplied the
superficial when the substantial was what had been needed.
Regrettably they had *fed* the deer but they had not *nourished*
them.

*When crises come in our
lives—and they will—the
philosophies of men
interlaced with a few
scriptures and poems just
won't do.*

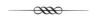

I love what President J. Reuben Clark said of our youth well
over a half century ago. The same thing can be said of new
members. "[They] are hungry for the things of the spirit;" he
said, "they are eager to learn the Gospel, and they want it

straight, undiluted. . . . You do not have to sneak up behind [them] and whisper religion in [their] ears; . . . you can bring these truths [out] openly."[7]

Satan is certainly not subtle in his teachings; why should we be? Whether we are instructing our children at home or standing before an audience in church, let us *never* make our faith difficult to detect. Remember—we are to be teachers "come from God" (John 13:13). Never sow seeds of doubt. Avoid self-serving performance and vanity. Prepare lessons well. Give scripturally based sermons. Teach the revealed doctrine. Bear heartfelt testimony. Pray and practice and try to improve. In our administrative meetings let us both "instruct and edify" as the revelations say, that even in these our teaching may ultimately be "from on high" (D&C 43:8, 16). The Church will be the better for it, and so will you, for as Paul said to the Romans, "Thou therefore which teachest another, teachest thou not thyself?" (Romans 2:21).

A memorable account of the power of such teaching comes from the life of the prophet Jeremiah. This great man felt the way most teachers or speakers or Church officers feel when called—inexperienced, inadequate, frightened. "Ah, Lord," he cried, "behold, I cannot speak: for I am [but] a child."

But the Lord reassured him: "Be not afraid of their faces: for I am with thee. . . . Therefore gird up thy loins, and arise, and speak unto them" (Jeremiah 1:6, 8, 17).

So speak unto them he did, but initially not with much success. Things went from bad to worse until finally he was imprisoned and made a laughingstock among the people. Angry that he had been so mistreated and maligned, Jeremiah vowed, in effect, never to teach another lesson, whether that be to an investigator, Primary child, new convert, or—heaven forbid—

the fifteen-year-olds. "I will not make mention of [the Lord], nor speak any more in his name," the discouraged prophet said. But then came the turning point of Jeremiah's life. Something had been happening with every testimony he had borne, every scripture he had read, every truth he had taught. Something had been happening that he hadn't counted on. Even as he vowed to close his mouth and walk away from the Lord's work, he found that he could not. Why? Because "his word was in mine heart as a burning fire shut up in my bones, and I was weary with forbearing, and I could not stay" (Jeremiah 20:7–9).

That is what happens in the gospel to both the teacher and the taught. It is what happened to Nephi and Lehi when, the book of Helaman says, "the Holy Spirit of God did come down from heaven, and did enter into their hearts, and they were filled as if with fire, and they could speak forth marvelous words" (Helaman 5:45). Surely it must have been that kind of heavenly joy Mary Magdalene experienced when near the Garden Tomb she unexpectedly beheld her beloved resurrected Lord and said to him simply, "Rabboni" (John 20:16; see footnote to Greek), which is to say, literally, "Teacher."

May we exalt the teaching experience within the home and within the Church and improve our every effort to edify and instruct. In all of our meetings and all of our messages may we nourish by the good word of God. And may our children and new converts, our neighbors and new friends, say of our honest efforts, "Thou art a teacher come from God."

NOTES

From a talk given at general conference, April 1998.

1. See Gordon B. Hinckley, "Converts and Young Men," *Ensign*, May 1997, 47.

2. *Teaching, No Greater Call* (Salt Lake City: The Church of Jesus Christ of Latter-day Saints, 1999); see also Spencer W. Kimball, "No Greater Call," Sunday School Conference, 1 October 1967.

3. In Conference Report, October 1916, 57.

4. *Teachings of Spencer W. Kimball,* ed. Edward L. Kimball (Salt Lake City: Bookcraft, 1982), 524; emphasis added.

5. "How to Be a Teacher When Your Role as a Leader Requires You to Teach," address given at General Authority Priesthood Board Meeting, 5 February 1969; emphasis added.

6. See John Taylor, *The Gospel Kingdom,* sel. G. Homer Durham (Salt Lake City: Deseret Book, 1943), 78.

7. "The Charted Course of the Church in Education," address given at Brigham Young University Summer School in Aspen Grove, Utah, 8 August 1938, 4, 9.

CHAPTER 8

THE TONGUE OF ANGELS

The Prophet Joseph Smith deepened our understanding of the power of speech when he taught, "It is by words . . . [that] every being works when he works by faith. God said, 'Let there be light: and there was light.' Joshua spake, and the great lights which God had created stood still. Elijah commanded, and the heavens were stayed for the space of three years and six months, so that it did not rain. . . . All this was done by faith. . . . *Faith, then, works by words; and with [words] its mightiest works have been, and will be, performed.*"[1] Like all gifts "which cometh from above," words are "sacred, and must be spoken with care, and by constraint of the Spirit" (D&C 63:64).

It is with this realization of the power and sanctity of words that I wish to caution us, if caution is needed, regarding how we speak to each other and how we speak of ourselves.

There is a line from the Apocrypha that puts the seriousness of this issue better than I can. It reads, "The stroke of the whip maketh marks in the flesh: but the stroke of the tongue breaketh the bones" (Ecclesiasticus 28:17).

With that stinging image in mind, I was particularly impressed to read in the book of James that there was a way I could be "a perfect man."

Said James: "For in many things we offend all. *[But] if any man offend not in word, the same is a perfect man,* and able also to bridle the whole body."

Continuing the imagery of the bridle, he writes: "Behold, we put bits in the horses' mouths, that they may obey us; and we turn about their whole body.

"Behold also the ships, which though they be so great, and are driven of fierce winds, yet are they turned about with a very small helm. . . ."

Then James makes his point: "The tongue is [also] a little member. . . . [But] behold, how great a [forest] a little fire [can burn].

" . . . So is the tongue [a fire] among our members, . . . it defileth the whole body, . . . it is set on fire of hell.

"For every kind of beasts, and of birds, and of serpents, and of things in the sea, . . . hath been tamed of mankind:

"But the tongue can no man tame; it is an unruly evil, full of deadly poison.

"Therewith bless we God, even the Father; and therewith curse we men, which are made after the similitude of God.

"Out of the same mouth proceedeth blessing and cursing. My brethren, these things ought not so to be" (James 3:2–10; emphasis added).

That is pretty straightforward! Obviously James doesn't mean our tongues are always iniquitous, nor that everything we say is "full of deadly poison." But he clearly means that at least some things we say can be destructive, even venomous—and that is a chilling indictment for a Latter-day Saint! The voice that bears profound testimony, utters fervent prayer, and sings the hymns of Zion *can be* the same voice that berates and criticizes, embarrasses and demeans, inflicts pain and destroys the spirit of oneself and of others in the process. "Out of the same mouth proceedeth blessing and cursing," James grieves. "These things ought not so to be."

Is this something we could all work on just a little? Is this an area in which we could each try to be a little more like a "perfect" man or woman?

If you are a husband, you have been entrusted with the most sacred gift God can give you—a wife, a daughter of God, the mother of your children who has voluntarily given herself to you for love and joyful companionship. Think of the kind things you said when you were courting, think of the blessings you have given with hands placed lovingly upon her head, think of yourself and of her as the god and goddess you both inherently are, and then reflect on other moments characterized by cold, caustic, unbridled words. Given the damage that can be done with our tongues, little wonder the Savior said, "Not that which goeth into the mouth defileth a man; but that which cometh out of the mouth, this defileth a man" (Matthew 15:11).

A husband who would never dream of striking his wife physically can break, if not her bones, then certainly her heart by the brutality of thoughtless or unkind speech. Physical abuse is uniformly and unequivocally condemned in The Church of Jesus Christ of Latter-day Saints. If it is possible to be more condemning than that, we speak even more vigorously against all forms of sexual abuse. Here, I speak against verbal and emotional abuse of anyone against anyone, but especially of husbands against wives. These things ought not to be.

Yet the sin of verbal abuse knows no gender. Wives, what of the unbridled tongue in *your* mouth, of the power for good or ill in *your* words? How is it that such a lovely voice, which by divine nature is so angelic, so close to the veil, so instinctively gentle and inherently kind, could ever in turn be so shrill, so biting, so acrid and untamed? A woman's words can be more piercing than any dagger ever forged, and they can drive the people she loves to retreat beyond a barrier more distant than anyone would ever have imagined when such a verbal exchange was beginning. There is no place in that magnificent spirit of yours for acerbic or abrasive expression of any kind, including gossip or backbiting or catty remarks. Let it never be said of our home or our ward or our neighborhood that "the tongue is a fire, a world of iniquity . . . [burning] among our members" (James 3:6).

May I expand this counsel to make it a full family matter. We must be so careful in speaking to a child. What we say or don't say, how we say it and when is so very, very important in shaping a child's view of himself or herself. But it is even more important in shaping that child's faith in us and in God. Be constructive in your comments to a child—always. Never tell children, even in whimsy, that they are fat or dumb or lazy or homely. You would never do that maliciously, but they remember and may struggle for years trying to forget—and to forgive. And try not to compare your children, even if you think you are skillful at it. You may say most positively that "Susan is pretty and Sandra is bright," but all Susan will remember is that she isn't bright and Sandra that she isn't pretty. Praise each child individually for what that child is, and help him or her escape our culture's obsession with comparing, competing, and never feeling we are "enough."

In all of this, I suppose it goes without saying that negative speaking so often flows from negative thinking, including negative thinking about ourselves. We see our own faults, we speak—or at least think—critically of ourselves, and before long that is how we see everyone and everything. No sunshine, no roses, no promise of hope or happiness. Before long we and all around us are miserable.

Praise each child individually for what that child is, and help him or her escape our culture's obsession with comparing, competing, and never feeling we are "enough."

I love what Elder Orson F. Whitney once said: "The spirit of the gospel is optimistic; it trusts in God and looks on the bright side of things. The opposite or pessimistic spirit drags men down and away from God, looks on the dark side, murmurs, complains, and is slow to yield obedience."[2] We should honor the Savior's declaration to "be of good cheer" (Matthew 14:27; Mark 6:50; John 16:33). (Indeed, it seems to me we may be more guilty of breaking that commandment than almost any other!) Speak hopefully. Speak encouragingly, including about yourself. Try not to complain and moan incessantly. As someone once said, "Even in the golden age of civilization someone undoubtedly grumbled that everything looked too yellow."

I have often thought that Nephi's being bound with cords and beaten by rods must have been more tolerable to him than listening to Laman and Lemuel's constant murmuring (see 1 Nephi 3:28–31; 18:11–15). Surely he must have said at least once, "Hit me one more time. I can still hear you." Yes, life has its problems and yes, there are negative things to face, but please accept one of Elder Holland's maxims for living—no misfortune is so bad that whining about it won't make it worse.

Paul put it candidly, but very hopefully. He said to all of us:

"Let no corrupt communication proceed out of your mouth, but [only] that which is good . . . [and] edifying, that it may minister grace unto the hearers.

No misfortune is so bad that whining about it won't make it worse.

"And grieve not the holy Spirit of God. . . .

"Let all bitterness, and wrath, and anger, and clamour, and evil speaking, be put away from you. . . .

"And be ye kind one to another, tenderhearted, forgiving one another, even as God for Christ's sake hath forgiven you" (Ephesians 4:29–32).

In his deeply moving final testimony, Nephi calls us to "follow the Son [of God], with full purpose of heart," promising that "after ye have . . . received the baptism of fire and of the Holy Ghost, [ye] can speak with a new tongue, yea, even with the tongue of angels. . . . And . . . how could ye speak with the tongue of angels save it were by the Holy Ghost? Angels speak by the power of the Holy Ghost; wherefore, they speak the words of Christ" (2 Nephi 31:13–14; 32:2–3). Indeed, Christ was and is "the Word," according to John the Beloved (John 1:1), full of grace and truth, full of mercy and compassion.

So, in this long eternal quest to be more like our Savior, may we try to be "perfect" men and women in at least this one way now—by offending not in word, or, more positively put, by speaking with a new tongue, the tongue of angels. Our words, like our deeds, should be filled with faith and hope and charity, the three great Christian imperatives so desperately needed in the world today. With such words, spoken under the influence of the Spirit, tears can be dried, hearts can be healed, lives can be elevated, hope can return, confidence can prevail.

Please know that your Father in Heaven loves you and so does His Only Begotten Son. When They speak to you—and They will—it will not be in the wind, nor in the earthquake, nor in the fire, but it will be with a voice still and small, a voice tender and kind (see 1 Kings 19:11–12). It will be with the tongue of angels. May we all rejoice in the thought that when we say edifying, encouraging things unto the least of these, our brethren and sisters and little ones, we say it unto God (see Matthew 25:40).

NOTES

From a talk given at general conference, April 2007.

1. Joseph Smith, *Lectures on Faith* (Salt Lake City: Deseret Book, 1985), lecture 7, paragraph 3, emphasis added.
2. In Conference Report, April 1917, 43.

CHAPTER 9

"Witnesses unto Me"

As the resurrected Jesus concluded His earthly ministry, He gave this paramount charge to His Apostles and those who would follow them:

"Go ye therefore, and teach all nations, baptizing them in the name of the Father, and of the Son, and of the Holy Ghost" (Matthew 28:19).

"Ye shall receive power, . . . and ye shall be witnesses unto me both in Jerusalem, and in all Judaea, and in Samaria, and unto the uttermost part of the earth" (Acts 1:8).

Remembering always to act with courtesy and propriety, we have a responsibility to be witnesses of Jesus Christ "at all times and in all things, and in all places" (Mosiah 18:9), to proclaim each in our own way the great cause to which Christ has called us. The twelve-hour-a-day, heavy-duty effort we can leave to the full-time missionaries, but why should they have all the fun? We are entitled to a seat at the abundant table of testimony as well, and fortunately a place has been reserved there for each member of the Church.

Indeed, one of the axioms of our day is that no mission or missionaries can ultimately succeed without the loving participation and spiritual support of the local members working with them in a balanced effort. Initial investigators may come from many different sources, but those who are actually baptized and who are firmly retained in activity in the Church come overwhelmingly from friends and acquaintances known to members of the Church.

As President Gordon B. Hinckley once said in a Churchwide broadcast:

"My heart reaches out to you missionaries. You simply cannot do it alone and do it well. You must have the help of others. That power to help lies within each of us. . . .

"Now, my brethren and sisters, we can let the missionaries try to do it alone, or we can help them. If they do it alone, they will knock on doors day after day and the harvest will be meager. Or as members we can assist them in finding and teaching investigators. . . .

"Brothers and sisters, all of you out in the wards and stakes and in the districts and branches, I invite you to become a vast army with enthusiasm for this work and a great overarching desire to assist the missionaries in the tremendous responsibility they have to carry the gospel to every nation, kindred, tongue, and people."[1]

I like the ring of those phrases "a vast army with enthusiasm for this work" and "a great overarching desire to assist the missionaries." Let me note a number of things we can do to respond to that call. You will recognize how many of them you are already doing.

Above all else we can live the gospel. Surely there is no more powerful missionary message we can send to this world than the example of a loving and happy Latter-day Saint life. The manner and bearing, the smile and kindness of a faithful member of the Church bring a warmth and an outreach that no missionary tract or videotape can convey. People do not join the Church because of what they know. They join because of what they feel, what they see and want spiritually. Our spirit of testimony and happiness in that regard will come through to others if we let it. As the Lord said to Alma and the sons of Mosiah, "Go forth . . . that ye may show forth good examples unto them in me, and I will make an instrument of thee in my hands unto the salvation of many souls" (Alma 17:11).

People do not join the Church because of what they know. They join because of what they feel, what they see and want spiritually.

A young returned missionary sister from Hong Kong told me that when she and her companion asked an investigator if she believed in God, the woman replied, "I didn't until I met a member of your church and observed how she lived." What exemplary missionary work! Asking every member to be a missionary is not nearly as crucial as asking every member to be a member! Thank you for living the gospel.

Thank you also for praying for the missionaries. *Everyone* prays for the missionaries. May it ever be so. In that same spirit, we should also pray for those who are (or who need to be) meeting the missionaries. In Zarahemla, members were commanded to "join in fasting and mighty prayer" (Alma 6:6) for those who had not yet joined the Church of God. We can do the same.

We can also pray daily for our own personal missionary experiences. Pray that under the divine management of such things, the missionary opportunity you want is already being prepared in the heart of someone who longs for and looks for what you have. "There are many yet on the earth . . . who are only kept from the truth because they know not where to find it" (D&C 123:12). Pray that they will find you! And then be alert, because there are multitudes in your world who feel a famine in their lives, "not a famine of bread, nor a thirst for water, but of hearing the words of the Lord" (Amos 8:11).

When the Lord delivers this person to your view, just chat—about anything. You can't miss. You don't have to have a prescribed missionary message. Your faith, your happiness, the very look on your face is enough to quicken the honest in heart. Haven't you ever heard a grandmother talk about her grand-children? That's what I mean—minus the photographs! The gospel will just tumble out. You won't be able to contain your-self!

But perhaps even more important than speaking is listen-ing. These people are not lifeless objects disguised as a baptismal statistic. They are children of God, our brothers and sisters, and they need what we have. Be genuine. Reach out sincerely. Ask these friends what matters most to them. What do they cher-ish, and what do they hold dear? And then listen. If the setting is right you might ask what their fears are, what they yearn for, or what they feel is missing in their lives. I promise you that something in what they say will always highlight a truth of the gospel about which you can bear testimony and about which you can then offer more. Elder Russell Nelson told me once that one of the first rules of medical inquiry is "Ask the patient where it hurts. The patient," he said, "will be your best guide to a correct diagnosis and eventual remedy." If we listen with love, we won't need to wonder what to say. It will be given to us—by the Spirit and by our friends.

For those who find it difficult to initiate missionary conversations—and many do—the Church's pass-along cards are a lovely, effortless way to let others know some of your basic beliefs and how they may learn more. For example, this is the easiest way I personally have yet found to offer people a copy of the Book of Mormon without my needing to carry a knapsack full of books as I travel.

Now let me increase the tempo of this message just a little. Many more of us can prepare for senior missionary service when that time in our life comes. As the senior couples at the MTC in Provo have said on a poster, "Let's lengthen our shuffle!" I just returned from a long trip that took me to half a dozen missions. Everywhere I went during those weeks, I found senior couples giving the most remarkable and rewarding leadership imaginable, providing stability, maturity, and experience that no nineteen-year-old or twenty-one-year-old could possibly be expected to provide. I found all kinds of couples, including a few former mission and temple presidents and their wives, who had come to parts of the world totally unknown to them to quietly, selflessly serve a second or a third or a fourth mission. I was deeply moved by every one of those people.

Elder and Sister John Hess of Ashton, Idaho, are one such couple. "We're just old potato farmers," John told me at a luncheon we attended together, but that is precisely what the nation of Belarus in the Russia Moscow Mission needed. For years the very best potato yields on government plots of ground there had been 50 sacks of potatoes a hectare. Considering it takes 22 sacks of seed to plant a hectare, the return was poor indeed. They needed help.

Brother Hess asked for ground just three feet away from the government plots, rolled up his sleeves, and went to work with the same seed, tools, and fertilizer available in Belarus. Come harvest time they began to dig, then called on others to dig, then called on everyone to dig. With the same rainfall and soil, but with an extra measure of Idaho industry, experience, and prayer, the plots planted by the Hesses produced a whopping 550 sacks per hectare—eleven times better than any prior yield on that land. At first no one would believe the difference. They wondered if secret teams had come in the night or if some wonder drug had been used. But it was none of that. Brother Hess said, "We needed a miracle, so we asked for one." Within a year, in that community young proselyting missionaries found much more success just because an "old potato farmer" from Idaho answered the call of his church.

There are all kinds of needs in this work, and there is a resolute missionary tradition of responding to the call to serve at every *age and in every circumstance.*

Most missionary couples serve much more routinely than that, employing their leadership experience in wards and branches, but the point is that there are all kinds of needs in this work, and there is a resolute missionary tradition of responding to the call to serve at *every* age and in every circumstance. I learned from one mission president that one of his young sister missionaries, nearing the end of her very faithful and successful mission, said through her tears that she must return home immediately. When he inquired as to the problem, she told him money had become so difficult for her family that to continue her support, the family had rented out their home and were using the rental proceeds to pay her mission expenses. For living accommodations, they had moved into a storage locker. For water, they used a neighbor's outdoor tap and hose; for a bathroom they went to a nearby gasoline station. This family, in which the father had recently passed away, were so proud of their missionary and so independent in spirit that they had managed to keep this recent turn of events from most of their friends and virtually all of their Church leaders.

When this situation was discovered, the family was restored to the home immediately. Long-term solutions to their economic circumstances were put in place, and the complete amount of remaining missionary support for their missionary daughter was secured overnight. With her tears dried and fears allayed, this faithful, hardworking young sister finished her mission triumphantly and was recently married in the temple to a wonderful young man.

In our blessed day we do not ask the kind of severe sacrifice this missionary family offered, but our generation has been the beneficiary of earlier generations who did sacrifice so very much in serving the missionary cause we declare. We can all do just a little more to pass that tradition on to those who follow us.

The Apostle John asked the Lord if he, John, might remain on the earth beyond the normal span of life for no other purpose than to bring more souls unto God. In granting that wish, the Savior said that this was "a greater work" and a nobler desire even than that of desiring to come into the presence of the Lord "speedily" (see D&C 7:4–5).

Like all prophets and Apostles, the Prophet Joseph Smith understood the deep meaning of John's request when he said, "After all that has been said, [our] greatest and most important duty is to preach the Gospel."[2] I bear witness of that gospel and of Jesus Christ, who embodied it. I testify that "the worth of souls is great in the sight of God" (D&C 18:10) and that saving those souls through the redeeming Atonement of His Beloved Son is at the very heart of His work and His glory (see Moses 1:39). In pursuing that work I testify with Jeremiah that this last great missionary declaration to modern Israel will, in the end, be a greater miracle than ancient Israel's crossing of the Red Sea (see Jeremiah 16:14–16). I pray that we will courageously and enthusiastically share the miracle of this message.

NOTES

From a talk given at general conference, April 2001.

1. "Find the Lambs, Feed the Sheep," *Ensign*, May 1999, 106, 107, 110.
2. *Teachings of the Prophet Joseph Smith*, sel. Joseph Fielding Smith (Salt Lake City: Deseret Book, 1976), 113.

CHAPTER 10

TERROR, TRIUMPH, AND A WEDDING FEAST

I address this chapter particularly to young adult readers in the context of ongoing anxiety in the world and some of the challenges we face at home and abroad. Of course, there have always been challenges in every age and dispensation, but on September 11, 2001, a violent and near-unimaginable event rocked the whole world, and the aftermath of that act has dramatically and perhaps permanently affected many of the ways in which the world now lives.

The citizens of the nations across the earth have, since that fateful day, been dangling off balance, have been made more fearful, and have been alarmed by international events and the almost wholesale use of the word *terror*. Not many years ago that word was reserved almost entirely for B-grade movie advertisements and Stephen King novels. Now, sadly, it is daily fare in our newspapers and so common in conversation that even young children, including the schoolchildren in Russia, are conscious that the world in which we live can be brutally, criminally affected by people called "terrorists." And there are other disasters of other kinds, natural and otherwise, documented in the news that remind us that life can be fragile, that life can present fateful turns of events.

Against that backdrop, I know that many of you have wondered in your hearts what all of this means regarding the end of the world and your life in it. Many have asked, "Is this the hour of the Second Coming of the Savior and all that is prophesied surrounding that event?" Indeed, sometime not long after 9/11, I had a missionary ask me in all honesty and full of faith, "Elder Holland, are these the last days?" I saw the earnestness in his face and some of the fear in his eyes, and I wanted to be reassuring. I thought perhaps an arm around him and some humor could relieve his anxiety a little. Giving him a hug, I said, "Elder, I may not be the brightest person alive, but even I know the name of the Church." We then talked about being Latter-day Saints. I said, "Yes, Elder, we are in the last days, but there is really nothing new about that. The promised Second Coming of the Savior began with the First Vision of the Prophet Joseph Smith in 1820. So we already have more than 180 years of experience seeing the Second Coming and the last days unfold. We can be certain that we are in the last days—years and years of them," I said, and gave him a friendly shake of the hand and sent him on his way.

He smiled, seemed more reassured to put all this in some context, and went on his way. I assume he has long since finished a successful mission and is now happily at home getting on with his life.

I hasten to say that I *do* know what this young man was really asking. What he really meant was, "Will I finish my mission? Is there any point in getting an education? Can I hope for a marriage? Do I have a future? Is there any happiness ahead for me?" And I say to you what I said years ago to him: "Yes, certainly—to all those questions."

As far as the actual timing of the final, publicly witnessed Second Coming itself and its earthshaking events, I do not know when that will happen. *No one* knows when it will happen. The Savior said that even the angels in heaven would not know (see Matthew 24:36).

We should watch for the signs and read the meaning of the seasons, we should live as faithfully as we possibly can, and we should share the gospel with everyone so that blessings and protections will be available to all. But we cannot and must not be paralyzed just because that event and the events surrounding it are out there ahead of us somewhere. We cannot stop living life. Indeed, we should live life more fully than we have ever lived it before. After all, this is the dispensation of the *fulness* of times.

I say this because in recent times—post 9/11 times, I suppose—I have heard very fearful and even dismal opinions coming from some in your age group regarding the questions that missionary had in mind. I have heard some of *you* say that *you* wonder whether there is any purpose in going on a mission or getting an education or planning for a career if the world we live in is going to be so uncertain. I have even heard sweethearts say, "We don't know whether we should get married in such uncertain times."

Worst of all, I have heard reports of some newlyweds questioning whether they should bring children into a terror-filled world on the brink of latter-day cataclysms. May I tell you that, in a way, those kinds of attitudes worry me more than Al-Qaeda worries me.

We must never, in any age or circumstance, let fear and the father of fear (Satan himself) divert us from our faith and faithful living. There have always been questions about the future. Every young person and every young couple in every era has had to walk by faith into what has always been some uncertainty—starting with Adam and Eve in those first tremulous steps out of the Garden of Eden. But that is all right. This is the plan. It will be okay. Just be faithful. God is in charge. He knows your name and He knows your need.

We must never, in any age or circumstance, let fear and the father of fear (Satan himself) divert us from our faith and faithful living.

Faith in the Lord Jesus Christ—that is the first principle of the gospel. We must go forward, as it says in K. Newell Dayley's hymn commemorating our pioneers of the past, "with faith in ev'ry footstep."[1] But like those pioneers, you do have to keep taking them—one step and then another and then the next. That is how tasks are accomplished, that is how goals are achieved, and that is how frontiers are conquered. In more divine language, that is how worlds are created and it is how *your* world will be created.

God expects you to have enough faith and determination and enough trust in Him to keep moving, keep living, keep rejoicing. In fact, He expects you not simply to *face* the future (that sounds pretty grim and stoic); He expects you to embrace and *shape* the future—to love it and rejoice in it and delight in your opportunities.

God is anxiously waiting for the chance to answer your prayers and fulfill your dreams, just as He always has. But He can't if you don't pray, and He can't if you don't dream. In short, He can't if you don't believe.

Drawing upon my vast background of children's bedtime stories, I say you can pick your poultry. Either you can be like Chicken Little and run about shouting, "The sky is falling; the sky is falling," or you can be like the Little Red Hen and forge ahead with the productive tasks of living, regardless of who does or doesn't help you or who does or doesn't believe just the way you believe.

So much for farmyard stories! How about two scriptures, both directed at those who live in perilous times?

The first is from section 101 of the Doctrine and Covenants. If you recall, this revelation came as the Saints who were gathered in Missouri were at the very height of their persecution. Mobs had driven them from their homes. Hostility, even hatred, followed them from county to county as they sought refuge. These frightened Saints lost land, livestock, clothing, furniture, crops, and a host of personal possessions. Threats of death were heard every day. I suppose, at its worst, this was the most difficult and dangerous time—may I say "terror-filled"— that the Church had ever known. Later on names like *Haun's Mill* and *Liberty Jail* would take their place in our vocabulary forever.

Yet in that frightening time the Lord said to His people:

"Let your hearts be comforted concerning Zion; for all flesh is in mine hands; be still and know that I am God.

"Zion shall not be moved out of her place, notwithstanding her children are scattered.

"They that remain, and are pure in heart, shall return, and

come to their inheritances, they and their children, with songs of everlasting joy, to build up the waste places of Zion—

"And all these things that the prophets might be fulfilled" (D&C 101:16–19).

So, my young friends, let your hearts be comforted concerning Zion. And remember the most fundamental definition of Zion we have ever been given: those who are "pure in heart" (D&C 97:21). If you will keep your hearts pure, you and your children and your grandchildren shall sing songs of everlasting joy as you build up Zion—and you shall not be moved out of your place.

The other verse I refer to is from the Savior, spoken to His disciples as He faced His crucifixion and as they faced fear, disarray, and persecution. Talk about troubled times! In His last collective counsel to them in mortality, and knowing full well what lay ahead for Him and for them, He said: "These things I have spoken unto you, that in me ye might have peace. In the world ye shall have tribulation: but be of good cheer; I have overcome the world" (John 16:33).

So, in a world of tribulation—and there will always be plenty of it—let's remember our faith. Let's recall the *other* promises and prophecies that have been given, all the reassuring ones, and let's live life more fully, with more boldness and courage than at any other time in our history.

Christ has overcome the world and made straight a path for us in the wilderness. He has said to us in our day: "Gird up your loins and be prepared. Behold, the kingdom is yours, and the enemy shall not overcome" (D&C 38:9). So let's gird up. Let's get some gusto into singing those songs of everlasting joy.

That leads directly to a related point I want to make regarding the day in which you and I live. In times of anxiety we tend to focus pretty much (like my young missionary friend did) on the "Latter-day" part of our Church's name.

Here I issue a call to you to concentrate on the "Saint" portion of that phrase. That is the element in our Church title that should be demanding our attention. Think of the blessings we enjoy. Think of the remarkable age in which we live. Think of the economic and educational, scientific and spiritual blessings we have that no other era or people in the history of the world have ever had, and then consider the responsibility we have to live worthily in our moment in time.

We are making our appearance on the stage of mortality in the greatest dispensation of the gospel ever given to mankind, and we need to make the most of it.

Note this affirmation from Wilford Woodruff in 1894. Perhaps I do not need to remind you of the staggering challenges President Woodruff faced. Those years here in the West were, I suppose, every bit as fearful in their own way as were the ones I described in Missouri: prophets in seclusion, Apostles in prison, fear (in President Woodruff's words) "that the whole nation" was turning against our people, preparing to "make war upon" the Church.[2]

We are making our appearance on the stage of mortality in the greatest dispensation of the gospel ever given to mankind, and we need to make the most of it.

Nevertheless, President Woodruff said in the midst of such troubles: "The Almighty is with this people. We shall have all the revelations that we will need, if we will do our duty and obey the commandments of God. . . . While I . . . live I want to do my duty. I want the Latter-day

Saints to do their duty. . . . Their responsibility is great and mighty. The eyes of God and all the holy prophets are watching us. This is the great dispensation that has been spoken of ever since the world began. We are gathered together . . . by the power and commandment of God. We are doing the work of God. . . . Let us fill our mission."[3]

And in our own day, President Gordon B. Hinckley taught: "We of this generation are the end harvest of all that has gone before. It is not enough to simply be known as a member of this Church. A solemn obligation rests upon us. Let us face it and work at it.

"We must live as true followers of the Christ, with charity toward all, returning good for evil, teaching by example the ways of the Lord, and accomplishing the vast service He has outlined for us.

"May we live worthy of the glorious endowment of light and understanding and eternal truth which has come to us through all the perils of the past. Somehow, among all who have walked the earth, we have been brought forth in this unique and remarkable season. Be grateful, and above all be faithful."[4]

It is interesting to me that in those two quotations, separated in time by more than a hundred years, our prophets have focused not on the terror of the times in which they lived and not on the ominous elements of the latter days, in which we are all living. Instead, they felt to speak of the opportunity and blessing, and above all the responsibility, to seize the privileges afforded us in this, the greatest of all dispensations. Let me repeat President Hinckley's words: "Through all the perils of the past . . . somehow, among all who have walked the earth, we have been brought forth in this unique and remarkable season. Be grateful, and above all be faithful."[5]

I don't know how all of that makes you feel, but suddenly any undue anxiety about the times in which we live dissipates for me, and I am humbled and spiritually thrilled, motivated at the opportunity we have been given. God is watching over His world, His Church, His leaders, and He is certainly watching over you. Let's just make sure we are the "pure in heart" (D&C 97:21) and that we *are* faithful. How blessed you will be. How fortunate your children and grandchildren will be.

Think about it. No earlier people down through the gospel ages—including our own parents, in many cases—have had anywhere near the blessings that you and I have been given.

Think of the help we have been given to take the light of the gospel to a darkened world. We have more than fifty thousand missionaries—obviously far more than in any other age in the history of the world since time began. And that number is repeated *every two years* by those going out to replace their predecessors! But we need even more. We have an LDS presence in some 170 countries. We publish our scriptures in more than a hundred languages.

No earlier people down through the gospel ages—including our own parents, in many cases—have had anywhere near the blessings that you and I have been given.

Over six thousand years or so ago there was one temple in the Old World (it was rebuilt two or three times, but it was always the same temple on the same mountain: Mount Moriah in Jerusalem) and two or three temples in Book of Mormon history, but now we live in a time when temples are multiplying so rapidly we can hardly keep up.

Add the miracle of the computer, which helps us document our family histories and systematically perform saving ordinances for the redemption of our dead. Add modern transportation, which allows the First Presidency, the Twelve, and other General Authorities to circle the globe and personally bear witness of the Lord to all of the Saints in all of the lands. Add that where we cannot go we can now "send," as the scriptures say, with satellite broadcasts (see D&C 84:62).

Add *all* the elements of education, science, technology, communication, transportation, medicine, nutrition, and revelation that surround us, and we begin to realize what the angel Moroni meant when he said repeatedly to the boy prophet Joseph Smith, quoting the Old Testament prophet Joel, that in the last days God would "pour out [His] spirit upon *all* flesh" and that the whole world, all humankind, would be blessed by the light coming in all fields of endeavor as part of the Restoration of the gospel of Jesus Christ (Joel 2:28; emphasis added; see also Joseph Smith—History 1:41).

We consider all these blessings that we have in our dispensation, and we pause to say to our Father in Heaven, "How *great* Thou art"[6] and "How *good* Thou art."

In fact, I have a theory about those earlier dispensations and the leaders, families, and people who lived then. I have thought often about them and the destructive circumstances that confronted them. They faced terribly difficult times and, for the most part, did *not* succeed in their dispensations. Apostasy and darkness eventually came to every earlier age in human history. Indeed, the whole point of the Restoration of the gospel in these latter days is that it had *not* been able to survive in earlier times and therefore had to be pursued in one last, triumphant age.

We know the challenges Abraham's posterity faced (and still do). We know of Moses' problems with an Israelite people who left Egypt but couldn't quite get Egypt to leave them. Isaiah was the prophet who saw the loss of the ten Israelite tribes to the north. Jeremiah, Ezekiel, and Daniel were all prophets of captivity. Peter, James, John, and Paul, the great figures of the New Testament, all saw apostasy creeping into their world almost before the Savior had departed and certainly while they themselves were still living. Think of the prophets of the Book of Mormon, living in a dispensation ending with such painful communication between Mormon and Moroni about the plight they faced and the nations they loved dissolving into corruption, terror, and chaos.

In short, apostasy and destruction of one kind or another were the ultimate fate of every general dispensation we have ever had down through time. But here's my theory. My theory is that those great men and women, the leaders in those ages past, were able to keep going, to keep testifying, to keep trying to do their best, not because they knew that *they* would succeed but because they knew that *you* would. I believe they took courage and hope not so much from their own circumstances as from yours—a magnificent collection of young adults like you gathered by the hundreds of thousands around the world in a determined effort to see the gospel prevail and triumph.

Moroni said once, speaking to those of us who would receive his record in the last days:

"Behold, the Lord hath shown unto me great and marvelous things concerning that which must shortly come, at that day when these things shall come forth among you.

"Behold, I speak unto you as if ye were present, and yet ye

are not. But behold, Jesus Christ hath shown you unto me, and I know your doing" (Mormon 8:34–35).

One way or another, I think virtually all of the prophets and early Apostles had their visionary moments of our time—a view that gave them courage in their own less-successful eras. Those early brethren knew an amazing amount about us. Prophets such as Moses, Nephi, and the brother of Jared saw the latter days in tremendously detailed vision. Some of what they saw wasn't pleasing, but surely all those earlier generations took heart from knowing that there would finally be one dispensation that would not fail.

I think virtually all of the prophets and early Apostles had their visionary moments of our time—a view that gave them courage in their own less-successful eras.

Ours, not theirs, was the day that caused them to sing and prophesy of victory. Ours is the day, collectively speaking, toward which the prophets have been looking from the beginning of time, and those earlier brethren are over there still cheering us on! In a very real way, *their* chance to consider themselves fully successful depends on *our* faithfulness and *our* victory. I love the idea of going into the battle of the last days representing Alma and Abinadi and what they pled for and representing Peter and Paul and the sacrifices they made. If you can't get excited about that kind of assignment in the drama of history, you can't get excited!

Let me add another element to this view of the dispensation that I think follows automatically. Because ours is the last and greatest of all dispensations, because all things will eventually

culminate and be fulfilled in our era, there is, therefore, one particular, very specific responsibility that falls to those of us in the
Church now that did not rest quite the same way on the shoulders of Church members in any earlier time. Unlike the Church
in the days of Abraham or Moses, Isaiah or Ezekiel, or even in
the New Testament days of James and John, *we have a responsibility to prepare the Church of the Lamb of God to receive the Lamb
of God*—in person, in triumphant glory, in His millennial role
as Lord of Lords and King of Kings. No other dispensation ever
had that duty.

In the language of the scriptures, we are the ones designated
in all of history who must prepare the bride for the advent of
the Bridegroom and be worthy of an invitation to the wedding
feast (see Matthew 25:1–12; 22:2–14; D&C 88:92, 96). Collectively speaking—whether it is in our lifetime or our children's
or our grandchildren's or whenever—we nevertheless have the
responsibility as a Church and as individual members of that
Church to be worthy to have Christ come to us, to be worthy
to have Him greet us, and to have Him accept and receive and
embrace us. The lives we present to Him in that sacred hour
must be worthy of Him!

So, setting aside fear of the future or concerns about the
dimensions of a backyard bomb shelter, I am filled with awe,
with an overwhelming sense of duty to prepare my life (and to
the extent that I can, to help prepare the lives of the members
of the Church) for that long-prophesied day, for that transfer of
authority, for the time when we will make a presentation of the
Church to Him whose Church it is.

I do know this: When Christ comes, the members of His
Church *must* look and act like members of His Church are *supposed* to look and act if we are to be acceptable to Him. We

must be doing His work and we must be living His teachings. He must recognize us quickly and easily as truly being His disciples. As President J. Reuben Clark Jr. once advised, our faith must *not* be difficult to detect.[7]

When Christ comes, the members of His Church must look and act like members of His Church are supposed to look and act if we are to be acceptable to Him.

Yes, if in that great, final hour we say we are believers, then we had surely better be demonstrating it. The Shepherd knows His sheep, and we must be known in that great day as His followers in deed as well as in word.

Surely that is why President Hinckley said: "It is not enough [for us, you and me, now, in our time] to simply be known as a member of this Church. . . . We must live as true fol-lowers of . . . Christ."[8]

Yes, my beloved young friends, these are the latter days, and you and I are to be the best Latter-day *Saints* we can. Put an emphasis on the last word there, please.

When will all of this finish? When shall Christ appear publicly, triumphantly, and the Millennium begin? I have already told you that I don't know. What I do know is that the initial moments of that event began more than 180 years ago. I do know that as a result of that First Vision and what has followed it, we live in a time of unprecedented blessings—blessings given to us for the purpose of living faithfully and purely so when the Bridegroom finally and triumphantly arrives, He can personally, justifiably bid us to the wedding feast.

Is there a happy future for you and your posterity in these

latter days? Absolutely! Most assuredly you have a beautiful future. All wedding feasts are happy occasions. Will there be difficult times when those ominous latter-day warnings and prophecies are fulfilled? Of course there will. There always have been. Be prepared. Will those who have built upon the great rock of Christ withstand such winds, such hail, and the mighty shafts in the whirlwind? You know that they will. You have it on good word. You have it on His word! That "rock upon which ye are built . . . is a sure foundation, a foundation whereon if men [and women] build they cannot fall" (Helaman 5:12).

I encourage you to live with confidence, optimism, faith, and devotion. Be serious about life's challenges, but not frightened or discouraged. Indeed, the only concern I would have us entertain is a very personal one: How can we live more fully, more faithfully, so that all the blessings of this great dispensation can be showered upon each one of us and upon those whose lives we touch?

This is the Church and kingdom of God on earth. Joseph Smith was a prophet and Thomas S. Monson is a prophet. Truth has been restored. You and I are fortunate enough to have been born when all of this knowledge and all of this safety are available to us.

I testify to you that God not only lives, He loves us. He loves you. Everything He does is for our good and our protection. There is evil and sorrow in the world, but there is no evil or harm in Him. He is our Father—a perfect father—and He will shelter us from the storm.

I testify not only that Jesus is the Christ, the Holy and Only Begotten Son of God, but that He lives, that He loves us, that on the strength and merit of His atoning sacrifice, we too will live eternally. He conquered death and hell for us, and He conquered fear in the same way.

"Fear not, little flock. . . . Look [to Christ] in every thought; doubt not, fear not" (D&C 6:34, 36).

NOTES

From an address given at a Church Educational System fireside for young adults at Brigham Young University, September 12, 2004.

1. "Faith in Every Footstep," *Ensign,* January 1997, 15.
2. Wilford Woodruff's diary, December 31, 1889, cited in James B. Allen and Glen M. Leonard, *The Story of the Latter-day Saints,* 2nd ed., rev. and enl. (Salt Lake City: Deseret Book, 1992), 420.
3. In James R. Clark, comp., *Messages of the First Presidency of The Church of Jesus Christ of Latter-day Saints,* 6 vols. (Salt Lake City: Bookcraft, 1965–1975), 3:258; see also Gordon B. Hinckley, in Conference Report, April 2004, 84–85.
4. In Conference Report, April 2004, 85.
5. In Conference Report, April 2004, 85.
6. See "How Great Thou Art," *Hymns of The Church of Jesus Christ of Latter-day Saints* (Salt Lake City: The Church of Jesus Christ of Latter-day Saints, 1985), no. 86; emphasis added.
7. See *The Charted Course of the Church in Education,* rev. ed. (Salt Lake City: The Church of Jesus Christ of Latter-day Saints, 1994), 3–7.
8. In Conference Report, April 2004, 85.

ALL THINGS ARE POSSIBLE

CHAPTER 11

WHEN THE CALL COMES

In 1849, just two years after the Saints had entered the Salt
Lake Valley, Parley P. Pratt led an expedition that worked
its way down the state following roughly the path that
Interstate 15 now takes from Salt Lake City down through
Cedar City and beyond. When they finally got far enough south
to see my homeland in St. George, it was a real catastrophe.
Dropping three thousand feet from the rim of the Great Basin
down to the convergence of the Virgin and the Santa Clara
Rivers, it was dry and sandy, volcanic and rugged. The scouts
were not impressed.

The journal says: "Passed through a rugged stony, . . . almost
indescribable country, thrown together in dreadful confusion. . . .

"A wide expanse of chaotic matter presented itself, consist-
ing of huge hills, [red] deserts, cheerless, grassless plains, per-
pendicular rocks, loose barren clay, . . . sandstone lying in

inconceivable confusion—[with] lava in every direction—in short, a country in ruins turned inside out, upside down by terrible convulsions in some former age."[1]

Now I ask you to freeze the frame right there, because that was among the easier moments of some of those first exploratory and colonization journeys. However rugged the land looked going south, it was a lot tougher to then look east past Orderville and Panguitch, past Tropic and Escalante to the wind-whipped, erosion-gutted cliffs and canyon wilderness of San Juan country. That was truly a no-man's land, filled with hangouts for outlaws, trouble with the Native Americans, and the threat to life and livestock if one ventured out there.

Leaders of the Church knew that even though taming that rough, unchartered corner of our present state would be difficult, nevertheless it should be done.

Leaders of the Church knew that even though taming that rough, unchartered corner of our present state would be difficult, nevertheless it should be done. The Brethren wanted to establish a mission to build up the kingdom of God and bring the word of God to any who would listen, including the Native Americans living there. In 1877, the Church called a conference in St. George to discuss the problem, with over one hundred specially invited, hardy prospective settlers in attendance. They discussed various exploration plans, but delayed any action because of the unexpected death of President Young that year.

Two years later, at the quarterly conference of the Parowan Stake, what would eventually total some 250 of our people, primarily from the Parowan and Cedar Valleys, accepted the call by President John Taylor to establish the San Juan Mission. With eighty wagons and nearly one thousand head of cattle and horses, they began to cut their way toward and through imposing, unexplored territory of snow-capped mountains and towering stone pinnacles.

Seeking the shortest route to the San Juan, those first explorers overcame one obstacle after another but soon faced the largest and most intimidating barrier of all—the impassable gulf of the Colorado River Gorge. Miraculously their weary scouts found a narrow slit in the canyon, a crevice running two thousand feet straight down the red cliffs to the Colorado River below. This lone, near-lethal "Hole in the Rock" seemed to offer the only possible passage to the eastern side.

For the most part the slice in the sandstone was too narrow for horses, or in some places too narrow even for a man or woman to pass through. Sheer drops of as much as seventy-five feet would seem to have made it impossible for a mountain sheep, let alone loaded wagons. But after having left Iron County the previous April, the hardy Saints were not going to turn back now, so with blasting powder and tools, working most of December and January of 1879–1880, they cut a precarious, primitive road into the face of the canyon precipice.

With this roadbed, such as it was, finished—some of it literally hung on pegs drilled into the canyon wall—the task was now to get the first forty wagons down the "Hole." The others, waiting back at Fifty-Mile Spring, would follow later.

They organized themselves in such a way that twenty men and boys would hold each wagon back with long ropes to slow its descent. The wheels were then brake-locked with chains, allowing them to slide but trying to avoid the catastrophe of the wheels actually rolling.

In one of the great moments of pioneer history, one by one the company took the wagons down the treacherous precipice. When, miracle of miracles, they reached the canyon floor they eagerly started to ferry across the river with a flatbed boat they had fashioned for that purpose. As it turned out, the Joseph Stanford Smith family were in the last wagon to descend that day.

Stanford Smith had systematically helped the preceding wagons down, but somehow in their one-by-one success and consequent disappearance, the others apparently forgot that Brother Smith's family would still need help as the tail-enders. Deeply disturbed that he and his family seemed abandoned, Stanford moved his team, wagon, and family to the edge of the precipice. The team was placed in front and a third horse was hitched *behind* the wagon to the rear axle. The Smiths stood for a moment and looked down the treacherous "Hole." Stanford turned to his wife and said, "I am afraid we can't make it."

She replied, "[We must] make it."

He said, "If we only had a few men to hold the wagon back we *might* make it."

Replied his wife, "*I'll* do the holding back."

A quilt was laid on the ground. There she placed her infant son in the care of her three-year-old Roy and five-year-old Ada. "Hold little brother 'til papa comes for [the] three of you," she said. Then positioning herself behind the wagon, Belle Smith grasped the reins of the horse hitched to the back of the rig. (Now, remember—she and that one horse are going to try to hold back what twenty men and boys had done for the other wagons.) Stanford started the team down the "Hole." The

102

wagon lurched downward. With the first jolt the rear horse and Sister Smith were literally catapulted into the air. Recovering, she hung back, pulling on the lines with all her strength and courage. A jagged rock cut a cruel gash in her leg from heel to hip. The horse behind the wagon fell to his haunches. The half-dead animal was literally dragged most of the way down the incline. That gallant woman, clothes torn, with a grievous wound, hung on to those lines with all her might and faith, and with her husband muscled that wagon the full length of the incline all the way to the river's edge.

On reaching the bottom, and almost in disbelief at their accomplishment, Stanford immediately raced the two thousand feet back up to the top of the cliff, fearful for the welfare of the children. When he climbed over the rim, there he saw his three children literally unmoved from the position their mother had placed them in. Carrying the baby, with the other two children clinging to him and to each other, he led them down the rocky crack to their anxious mother below. At that point, in the distance they saw five men moving toward them carrying chains and ropes. The Smiths had been missed from the larger party. Realizing the plight they were in, these men were coming to help. Stanford called out, "Forget it, fellows. . . . [Belle] here is all the help a [man] needs [to make this journey]."[2]

"Of all places on the earth, why the Muddy?"

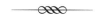

The Hole-in-the-Rock expedition is one of the more dramatic of all our local pioneer stories, but it is only one of many examples of the determination and devotion of the early Saints to answer the call of their prophet when it came. Another case in point is the creation of and call to the Muddy Mission. As with so many of those early pioneer settlements, the Muddy promised only a very hard life, and much soul-searching was done when the calls came to settle there. As one pioneer said, "Of all places on the earth, why the Muddy?"

Well, there actually were reasons. First of all, the Civil War had given rise to the possibility of shipping commodities via the Colorado River. For that purpose Call's Landing had been established on that river in 1864. Second, when the war interrupted traditional sources for textiles, the Cotton Mission had been established in St. George and Washington not too many miles away. It was assumed that cotton for that mill could be grown in the Muddy region. Third, the Latter-day Saints felt strongly their obligation to work with the Native American tribes in the region—helping to feed them, hoping to educate them, and wanting very much to remind them of their ancient scriptural heritage.

But, with all that, the region was nevertheless a lonely, barren wasteland. It seemed to have almost nothing to offer but heat and hard work. It was isolated, for the most part desolate, and the river that gave the mission its identity was aptly named. Almost everyone echoed that first observation, "Of all places on the earth, why the Muddy?"

I am not sure I can say "why" any better than President Brigham Young tried to say it, but as to "how" and with what faith and determination it was done, I can best let one of their own say it. It is so representative of the grit and spunk and moral conviction that both young and old had, and in this case especially the young.

Listen to the words of Elizabeth Claridge McCune, who wrote of her father's call to go settle the Muddy:

"No place on earth seemed so precious to me at fifteen years of age as dear old Nephi [in Utah's Juab County]. How eagerly we looked forward to the periodical visits of President Brigham Young and his company! Everything was done that could be thought of for their comfort and entertainment. And with all it was a labor of love.

"We went out with our Sabbath Schools and all the other organizations, with bands of music and flags and banners and flowers to meet and greet our beloved leader and his company. On one occasion the people were lined up on each side of the street waiting for the carriages to pass. Among them were twenty-five young ladies dressed in white who had strewn evergreens and wild flowers along the path. Brother Brigham, [Brother] Kimball and [Brother] Wells with [their] entire company got out of their carriages, and walked over the flowery road . . . to our homes, [where] dinner was prepared and served.

"We all attended the afternoon meeting, the girls in white having reserved seats in front. The sermons were grand, and we were happy until President Young announced that he had a few names to read of men who were to be called and voted in as mis-

"I know that my father will go and that nothing could prevent him, and I should not own him as a father if he would not go when he is called."
(Elizabeth Claridge)

sionaries to go and settle . . . the 'Muddy.' This almost stilled the beating of the hearts of all present. Many of our people had been called to go to settle the Dixie country—but the Muddy, so many miles farther south! And so much worse! Oh! Oh! I did not hear another name except 'Samuel Claridge.' Then how I sobbed and cried, regardless of the fact that the tears were spoiling [my] new white dress. The father of the girl who sat next to me was also called. Said my companion, 'What is [it] you [are] crying about? It doesn't make me cry. I know my father won't go.' 'Well, there is the difference,' said I. 'I know that my father *will* go and that nothing could prevent him, and I should not own him as a father if he would not go when he is called.' Then, I broke down sobbing again. . . .

"[And to realize] we had just moved into a new house and were fixed [so] comfortably. Many of our friends tried to persuade father to keep his home and farm; to go south a while and then come back. But father knew that this was not the kind of mission upon which he had been called. 'I will sell everything I own,' said he, 'and take my means to help build up another waste place in Zion.'"[3]

What is it that bred then and breeds now the loyalty and devotion found in this fifteen-year-old child and the family into which she was born? What is it that made her turn on her slightly less stalwart friend and declare (without a word of conversation with her parents!), "Well, there is the difference. I know that my father *will* go and that nothing could prevent him"? Where does that kind of spunk come from that would also go on to say, "And I should not own him as a father if he would not go when he is called"?

Nor does it seem to matter that all of this is blurted out amidst the unrestrained tears and sobbings of a teenager who has probably enjoyed her last new, white dress for a while.

What are we seeing in these two examples of faithful groups of pioneers? Well, it is what we have seen down through the dispensations of time and certainly down through this dispensation.

We are seeing what we saw when the Saints fled New York and Pennsylvania and Ohio and Missouri, then fled their beloved Nauvoo across an ice-bound river with the temple burning in the distance. It is what we saw when those same people buried their dead in large numbers at Winter Quarters, followed by isolated graves, sometimes as tiny as a bread box, near Chimney Rock or at one of the many crossings of the Sweetwater, or in a snow bank at Martin's Cove.

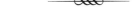

What we saw then and what we see now among the blessed Saints the world over is faith in God. Faith in the Lord Jesus Christ. Faith in the Prophet Joseph Smith. Faith in the reality of this work and the truthfulness of this message. It was faith that took a boy into a grove of trees to pray and it was faith that enabled him to get up off his knees, place himself in God's hands for the restoration of the gospel, and ultimately march toward his own martyrdom scarcely two dozen short years just ahead of him.

Faith always has been and always will be the first and abiding principle of the gospel and of our work.

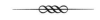

Little wonder that faith always has been and always will be the first and abiding principle of the gospel and of our work. It is the heart of our conviction not only that the work should go forth but that it can and will and must go forth.

I don't know how else mothers and fathers could leave those babies in those makeshift graves on the plains, then with one last look weep their way forward toward Zion. I don't know how else a woman like Belle Smith could sit her children at the edge of a cliff and muscle her wagon down the perilous incline. I don't know how else a Samuel Claridge could sell all he owned and head off to build Zion in the desolate Muddy Mission. The fundamental driving force in these stories is faith—rock-ribbed, furnace-refined, event-filled, spiritually girded faith that this is the truth, the very Church and kingdom of God, that when you are called you go.

There are still those "waste places of Zion" to be built up that old Brother Claridge spoke of, and there will always be a young generation like fifteen-year-old Elizabeth who will need to see such faith in action, from prophets at some distance (maybe even most of the time on a television screen) or from parents and leaders and friends very much closer to home who feel the same things, who know the same truths, who have the same faith.

Nurture your own physical and spiritual strength so that you have a deep reservoir of faith to call upon when tasks or challenges or demands of one kind or another come.

And so I issue this call to our faith, to the conviction we all must have burning in our hearts that this is the work of God and requires the best we can give to the effort. My first appeal is to each of you individually to nurture your own physical and spiritual strength so that you have a deep reservoir of faith to call upon when tasks or challenges or demands of one kind or another come. Pray and study, fast appropriately, search your soul and search the heavens for the testimony that led our pioneer parents. Then, when you need to reach down inside a little deeper and a little farther to face life and do your work, you will be sure there is something down there deeper and farther to call upon. As TV's Mister

Rogers once said of people, so say we of testimonies. "They should be simple and deep, not complex and superficial."

When you have your own faith, then you are prepared to bless your family. The single strongest indicator of activity and service, of devotion and loyalty in this Church continues to be the presence of strong family ties. I say that knowing full well that part of the majesty of this Church is in the *individual* member. Sometimes that is a new convert, sometimes that is one who is the only member of the Church in the family. Some individual somewhere has had to plant the flag of faith and start a new generation in the gospel. But the fact is that faith is better nurtured and more protected and longer lasting when there is an entire family to reinforce it. So after standing alone if you have to, work diligently to see that others in your family *don't* stand alone. Build your family and see that faith is strong there.

With that accomplished, then we can serve the Church near at hand or at some distant outpost if called. Then we can search out that lost sheep, member or nonmember, living or dead. This can only be done wisely and well when the other ninety-nine lambs, including our own little flock, are safely folded while we search. But if we have loved and taught those at home, they will understand exactly as little Elizabeth Claridge did: When the call comes you can be certain that my dad and mom, my brothers and my sisters are going to go.

There is work to be done. We cannot say that everyone has faith, that everyone has a strong family, that everyone has heard the gospel message and become believing, teaching, temple-going Latter-day Saints. No, there is a great amount of work yet to be done and I know this. The only way it will be done is through people like Stanford and Belle Smith, people like Samuel Claridge and his spunky daughter Elizabeth. The only way it will happen is with faith in this work, faith in what all believers are called to do, faith in the Lord Jesus Christ.

NOTES

Adapted from addresses given at an eastern and southern Utah stake conference broadcast, November 4, 2007, and at a Nevada stake conference broadcast, March 4, 2007.

1. Milton R. Hunter, *Brigham Young the Colonizer* (Salt Lake City, Deseret News Press, 1940), 47.

2. See David E. Miller, *Hole-in-the-Rock: An Epic in the Colonization of the Great American West* (Salt Lake City: University of Utah Press, 1959), 101–18; emphasis added.

3. *Young Woman's Journal*, July 1898, 292–93.

CHAPTER 12

CONTINUING IN PRAYER

I n August of 1861, only four months after the beginning of the Civil War, President Abraham Lincoln issued a proclamation for a day of public penitence, fasting, prayer and thanksgiving. Thursday was intentionally chosen as the day of national prayer because it could not be identified with any existing worshipping group. This proclamation for a day of prayer would be the first of nine such calls to national prayer issued over the course of Lincoln's forty-nine months in the presidency.

Today, our nation does not face a civil war with brother fighting brother in officially issued blue and gray uniforms. But we are plagued by brother fighting brother with handguns in university dormitories and college classrooms; with brutality in rural villages and in urban centers; with drunk-driven vehicles on city streets and interstate highways; and with hate-filled talk on public airwaves and private DVDs.

The 1861 proclamation stated: "It is fit and becoming in all people, at all times, to acknowledge and revere the Supreme Government of God; to bow in humble submission to his chastisements; to confess and deplore their sins and transgressions in the full conviction that the fear of the Lord is the beginning of wisdom; and to pray, with all fervency and contrition, for the pardon of their past offences, and for a blessing upon their present and prospective action."[1]

Surely we need to humbly seek the will of God in prayer just as did the Americans of Abraham Lincoln's day.

Mother Teresa wrote of prayer, "God has created us to love and to be loved, and this is the beginning of prayer—to know that he loves me, that I have been created for greater things." I believe we have all been created for "greater things" than we can comprehend. The times call for great things, but great things in the noblest and most redemptive sense are predicated upon tolerance, love, respect, understanding, dignity, prayer, God.

The Apostle Paul taught important principles relating to tolerance and love. To the Romans, he wrote: "Let love be without dissimulation. Abhor that which is evil; cleave to that which is good. Be kindly affectioned one to another . . . rejoicing in hope; patient in tribulation; continuing instant in prayer"

I believe we have all been created for greater things than we can comprehend. The times call for great things, but great things in the noblest and most redemptive sense are predicated upon tolerance, love, respect, understanding, dignity, prayer, God.

(Romans 12:9–12). President James E. Faust, in his final conference address, told the sad but inspiring story of how the Amish people reacted when a thirty-two-year-old milk truck driver stormed into an Amish school and shot ten girls, killing five and wounding five. Then he took his own life. I quote:

"This shocking violence caused great anguish among the Amish but no anger. There was hurt but no hate. Their forgiveness was immediate. Collectively they began to reach out to the milkman's suffering family. As the milkman's family gathered in his home the day after the shootings, an Amish neighbor came over, wrapped his arms around the father of the dead gunman, and said, 'We will forgive you.' Amish leaders visited the milkman's wife and children to extend their sympathy, their forgiveness, their help, and their love. About half of the mourners at the milkman's funeral were Amish. In turn, the Amish invited the milkman's family to attend the funeral services of the girls who had been killed. A remarkable peace settled on the Amish as their faith sustained them during this crisis.

There is no place in our homes or our society for acerbic or abrasive expression of any kind, including gossip or backbiting or catty remarks.

"One local resident very eloquently summed up the aftermath of this tragedy when he said, 'We were all speaking the same language, and not just English, but a language of caring, a language of community, [and] a language of service. And, yes, a language of forgiveness.'"[2]

Surely here was "love without dissimulation" and "patience

in tribulation." There was a great "evil to abhor" here but they chose to "cleave to that which was good." Surely they were "kindly affectioned one to another" and their triumph came because they were "instant in prayer."

Paul continues, "Bless them which persecute you: bless, and curse not" (Romans 12:14). Unfortunately, the places we hear cursing of our fellow man are not limited to the interior of our cars from road rage, or on athletic fields from hot-headed opponents or in the workplace from perceived slights by our employer. No, too often in today's society, we hear cursing in our homes and cursing of those we love. There is no place in our homes or our society for acerbic or abrasive expression of any kind, including gossip or backbiting or catty remarks.

In continuing with Paul's epistle: "Recompense to no man evil for evil. . . . If it be possible, as much as lieth in you, live peaceably with all men" (Romans 12:17–18). Too often in today's society, we seek revenge: Hezbollah vows to retaliate for Israeli incursions; Israel vows to do the same in reply; the ad for a TV program declares a gunman seeks revenge for the death of his sister; a major league baseball pitcher beats a batter to retaliate for a batter on his team being hit by a pitch.

In his classic novel *Les Miserables*, Victor Hugo illustrates in the life of Jean Valjean the principle of returning good for evil. You know the story. Jean Valjean, after spending nineteen years in prison and in the galleys for stealing a loaf of bread and for several attempts to escape, is finally released, but his past keeps haunting him. In the streets, he is repeatedly refused shelter for the night. Only the saintly Bishop, Monseigneur Myriel, welcomes him. Valjean repays his host's hospitality by stealing his silverware. When the police bring him back, the Bishop protects his errant guest by pretending that the silverware is a gift.

With a pious lie, he convinces them that the convict has promised to reform. Jean Valjean is forever changed by the Bishop's act of kindness in the face of his treachery.

Much later in the story, Jean Valjean himself exemplifies such grace. His lifelong nemesis, Inspector Javert, enters a fortress and is captured by the young defenders, then sentenced to death. Valjean volunteers to execute Javert. Instead, he spares the inspector's life and sends him away. He trusts God to be the ultimate judge.

The conduct of both Bishop Myriel and Jean Valjean adheres to Paul's counsel of, "Be not overcome of evil, but overcome evil with good" (Romans 12:21). Consider how much happier our modern communities would be if we served rather than sued.

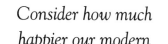

Consider how much happier our modern communities would be if we served rather than sued.

Now a word about prayer. Human beings are naturally drawn to prayer, which can be seen every day at the Wailing Wall in Jerusalem, at a mosque in Mecca, at a Buddhist temple in Bangkok, or at a Christian chapel anywhere in America. But it is not so natural to pray for one's enemy. In the midst of Hitler's Nazi regime, two German individuals with very different backgrounds and faiths show us how not to be overcome with evil, how not to let evil canker our prayers and our souls.

Edith Stein was a woman of Jewish birth who became an atheist by age fourteen, earned a doctorate degree, later converted to Catholicism at age thirty, then wrote a number of theological treatises including "The Prayer of the Church." At age forty-two, Edith entered the Carmel of Cologne as a nun, and four years later fled to the Carmel at Echt (Holland) to escape Nazi persecution of Jews. While in Holland she wrote: "The thought that we have . . . no lasting home is always with me. I have no other wish than that God's Will should be accomplished in me. How long I am to be here depends on Him. As to what will happen then, it is not for me to concern myself. But it is necessary to pray much, in order to remain faithful come what may."[3] At age fifty-one she was arrested, transported to Auschwitz, and executed in August 1942 for faithfulness to her Jewish heritage and opposition to the Nazi cause. Edith—now beatified and known to Catholics as Saint Teresa Benedicta of the Cross—was seen peacefully praying and actively serving her fellowman in the concentration camp until her last moments.

Dietrich Bonhoeffer was a Lutheran pastor, theologian, and participant in the Nazi resistance movement. Bonhoeffer wrote: "I can no longer condemn or hate a brother for whom I pray, no matter how much trouble he causes me. His face, that hitherto may have been strange and intolerable to me, is transformed into the countenance of a brother for whom Christ died, the face of a forgiven sinner."[4] He was arrested in 1943 and hanged at age thirty-nine in April 1945 at the Flossenbürg concentration camp. The prison doctor noted that Pastor Bonhoeffer said a short prayer before going to the gallows. The doctor stated, "I have hardly ever seen a man die so entirely submissive to the will of God."[5]

Even in the midst of great trial and persecution, Edith Stein, Dietrich Bonhoeffer, and untold others down through the ages of time have remained true to Paul's admonition of "continuing instant in prayer."

I close with a reference to the Sermon on the Mount,

undoubtedly the basic source for Paul's message to the Romans, for we hear so much of the one echoing in the other.

Matthew 5:48 concludes with that wonderfully staggering injunction from Jesus which seems so far beyond our reach— "Be ye therefore perfect, even as your Father which is in heaven is perfect." Surely this is the ultimate in spirituality and religiosity—to strive to approach the perfection of God.

If this comes as the grand finale, the great summation in a chapter that began with the sweet and simple Beatitudes, what immediately *precedes* perfection? Or better yet, what preparatory virtues point us toward perfection and this full majesty of God?

I quote the verses immediately prior to the grand declaration of perfection:

"Ye have heard that it hath been said, Thou shalt love thy neighbour, and hate thine enemy.

"But I say unto you, Love your enemies, bless them that curse you, do good to them that hate you, and pray for them which despitefully use you, and persecute you;

To make headway in a world of woe, we need to broaden our circle of love and lengthen the table of contents in our prayers.

"That ye may be the children of your Father which is in heaven: for he maketh his sun to rise on the evil and on the good, and sendeth rain on the just and on the unjust.

"For if ye love them which love you, what reward have ye? do not even the publicans the same?

"And if ye salute your brethren only, *what do ye more than others?* do not even the publicans so?" (Matthew 5:43–47; emphasis added).

I confess that I do not know how we meet the Savior's injunction to be perfect, but I am guessing we will be a lot closer to that goal if we can love our enemies, bless them that curse us, and pray for them that despitefully use us. Surely if we salute our friends only, what do we more than others? To make headway in a world of woe, we need to broaden our circle of love and lengthen the table of contents in our prayers.

I close with the words of Abraham Lincoln's July 7, 1864, prayer proclamation offered one year after the terrors of Gettysburg. His words still apply to us in an often violent and abusive world 143 years later.

Lincoln asked his fellow citizens to pray earnestly to the Almighty God and "to implore Him, as the Supreme Ruler of the World, not to destroy us as a people, nor suffer us to be destroyed by the hostility or connivance of other Nations, or by obstinate adhesion to our own counsels, which may be in conflict with His eternal purposes, and to implore Him to enlighten the mind of the Nation to know and do His will; humbly believing that it is in accordance with His will that our place should be maintained as a united people among the family of nations."[6]

I pray that we may we be willing to give God our hearts, our tongues, our hands, our prayers, and our whole souls as we live together in communities united in the bonds of greater understanding, deeper respect, and much more love.

NOTES

From an address given at a National Day of Prayer Service in the Provo Tabernacle, May 4, 2007.

1. *The Collected Works of Abraham Lincoln*, 9 vols., ed. Roy P. Basler (New Jersey: Rutgers University Press, 1953), 4:482.

2. James E. Faust, "The Healing Power of Forgiveness," *Ensign*, May 2007, 67.

3. "St Teresa Benedicta of the Cross, Edith Stein, Help Fellowship, Inc. http://www.helpfellowship.org/Edith_Stein_now_a_saint.htm

4. Dietrich Bonhoeffer, *Life Together* (New York: Harper, 1954), 86.

5. Eberhard Bethge, *Dietrich Bonhoeffer: Eine Biographie* (Munich: Christian Kaiser Verlag), 1037–38.

6. *Collected Works of Abraham Lincoln*, 7:431.

CHAPTER 13

"LIKE A WATERED GARDEN"

Surely and steadily The Church of Jesus Christ of Latter-day Saints moves across the earth. In Daniel's language it is "the stone . . . cut out of the mountain without hands" (Daniel 2:45). Isaiah described what he foresaw as "a marvellous work and a wonder" (Isaiah 29:14). It *is* a wonder! The restoration of the gospel of Jesus Christ is filled with miracles, revelations, manifestations of every kind. Many of those have come in our lifetime.

I was seventeen years old before there was any stake of Zion anywhere outside North America. There are now well over 1,000 stakes on those distant continents and isles of the sea. Dozens of temples have been built outside the United States; again, I was nearly fifteen before there was even one temple beyond the states and provinces of the USA and Canada.

We have lived to see the revelation extending the priesthood to all worthy males of appropriate age, a blessing that has accelerated the work in many parts of the world. We have lived to see the publication of our scriptures, wholly or in part, in nearly 100 languages.

We have lived to see the long-awaited creation of the Quorums of the Seventy with great men drawn from many nations and, in turn, deployed to serve in many nations. President Gordon B. Hinckley announced a Perpetual Education Fund that has the potential to bless many in even the most distant locations of the earth eventually. And so the internationalizing of the Church goes on.

I give this brief summary to highlight another miracle, another revelation, if you will, that may have been overlooked by the general membership of the Church. In a way it was intended to be transparent to the public eye. I speak of the decision made by the Brethren over a decade ago to cease placing any special assessments or other fund-raising obligations upon the members of the Church at home or abroad.

Inasmuch as this decision was made amidst the very international growth I have just described, how could this be done financially? How could we go to more and more distant locations at the very moment we were removing all ancillary assessments from our people? Logic in the situation might have suggested exactly the opposite course of action.

How was it done? I will tell you how it was done—with the wholehearted belief on the part of the presiding Brethren that the Lord's principles of tithing and freewill offerings would be honored by even the newest member of the Church and that loyalty to such divine principles would see us through.

I was not in the Quorum of the Twelve when that momentous decision was made, but I can imagine the discussions that were held and the act of faith required within the presiding councils of the Church. What if the Brethren were to cease assessments and the Saints did *not* pay their tithes and offerings? What then? So far as I know, that thought was never seriously entertained. They went forward in faith—faith in God, faith in revealed principle, faith in us. They never looked back. That was a magnificent (if nearly unnoticed) day in the maturing of The Church of Jesus Christ of Latter-day Saints.

But to honor that decision, we must be equally mature as individual members of the Church. May I then suggest five reasons why all of us, rich or poor, longtime member or newest convert, should faithfully pay our tithes and offerings.

First, do so for the sake of your children and grandchildren, the rising generation, who could now, if we are not careful, grow up in the Church with absolutely no understanding as to how their temples, chapels, seminaries, and socials are provided. Teach your children that many of the blessings of the Church are available to them because you and they give tithes and offerings to the Church. Teach them that those blessings could come virtually no other way.

Teach your children that many of the blessings of the Church are available to them because you and they give tithes and offerings to the Church.

Then take your children to tithing settlement with you, just as President Howard W. Hunter's grandson was taken with his father several years ago. In that experience the bishop indicated his pleasure in young Brother Hunter's wanting to pay a full tithing. In the process of receiving the coins, he asked the lad if he thought the gospel were true. As the boy handed over his full tithing of fourteen cents, this seven-year-old said he guessed the gospel was true but "it sure costs a lot of money."[1] Well, the buildings, programs, and materials I have mentioned do have an attached cost. That is not an unimportant lesson for our children to learn in their youth.

Second, pay your tithing to rightfully claim the blessings promised those who do so. "Prove me now herewith, saith the Lord of hosts, if I will not open you the windows of heaven, and pour you out a blessing, that there shall not be room enough to receive it" (Malachi 3:10). President Thomas S. Monson has taught, "The honest payment of tithing provides a person the inner strength and commitment to comply with the other commandments."[2]

After she lost her husband in the martyrdom at Nauvoo and made her way west with five fatherless children, Mary Fielding Smith continued in her poverty to pay tithing. When someone at the tithing office inappropriately suggested one day that she should not contribute a tenth of the only potatoes she had been able to raise that year, she cried out to the man, "William, you ought to be ashamed of yourself. Would you deny me a blessing? If I did not pay my tithing, I should expect the Lord to withhold His blessings from me. I pay my tithing, not only because it is a law of God, but because I expect a blessing by doing it. [I *need* a blessing.] By keeping this and other laws, I expect to . . . be able to provide for my family."[3]

I can't list all the ways that blessings will come from obedience to this principle, but I testify many will come in spiritual ways that go well beyond economics. In my life, for example, I have seen God's promise fulfilled that He would "rebuke the devourer for [my sake]" (Malachi 3:11). That blessing of protection against evil has been poured out upon me and on my loved ones beyond any capacity I have to adequately acknowledge. But I believe that divine safety has come, at least in part, because of our determination, individually and as a family, to pay tithing.

Pay your tithing as a declaration that possession of material goods and the accumulation of worldly wealth are not *the uppermost goals of your existence.*

Third, pay your tithing as a declaration that possession of material goods and the accumulation of worldly wealth are *not* the uppermost goals of your existence. As one young husband and father, living on a student budget, recently told me, "Perhaps our most pivotal moments as Latter-day Saints come when we have to swim directly against the current of the culture in which we live. Tithing provides just such a moment. Living in a world that emphasizes material acquisition and cultivates distrust for anyone or anything that has designs on our money, we shed that self-absorption to give freely, trustingly, and generously. By this act, we say—indeed—that we are different, that we are God's peculiar people. In a society that tells us money is our most important asset, we declare emphatically it is not."

President Spencer W. Kimball once spoke of a man who prided himself on his vast acreage and remarkable holdings—groves and vineyards, herds and fields, ponds and homes and possessions of every kind. He prided himself on these, but to the end of his life was unwilling to tithe on them or even acknowledge that they were gifts from God. President Kimball then spoke at the man's funeral, noting that this land baron was laid to rest in an oblong piece of soil measuring "the length of a tall man, the width of a heavy one."[4] In answer to the age-old question, "How much did he leave?" be reassured the answer will always be, "All of it." So we would do well to lay up treasures in heaven, where not taxes but doctrines give meaning to words like *estate, inheritance, testament,* and *will* (see Matthew 6:19–21).

Fourth, pay your tithes and offerings out of honesty and integrity because they are God's rightful due. Surely one of the most piercing lines in all of scripture is Jehovah's thundering inquiry, "Will a man rob God?" And we ask, "Wherein have we robbed thee?" He answers, "In tithes and offerings" (Malachi 3:8).

Paying tithing is *not* a token gift we are somehow charitably bestowing upon God. Paying tithing is discharging a debt. Elder James E. Talmage once described this as a contract between us and the Lord. He imagined the Lord saying: "'You have need of many things in this world—food, clothing, and shelter for your family . . ., the common comforts of life. . . . You shall have the means of acquiring these things; but remember they are mine, and I require of you the payment of a rental upon that which I

We would do well to lay up treasures in heaven, where not taxes but doctrines give meaning to words like estate, inheritance, testament, *and* will.

give into your hands. However, your life will not be one of uniform increase . . . [so] instead of doing as mortal landlords do—requir[ing] you to . . . pay in advance, whatever your fortunes or . . . prospects may be—you shall pay me . . . [only] when you have received; and you shall pay me in accordance with what you receive. If it so be that in one year your income is abundant, then . . . [your 10 percent will be a] little more; and if it be so that the next year is one of distress and your income is not what it was, then . . . [your 10 percent will be] less. . . . [Whatever your circumstance, the tithe will be fair.]'

"Have you ever found a landlord on earth who was willing to make that kind of [equitable] contract with you?" Elder Talmage asked. "When I consider the liberality of it all," he said, " . . . I feel in my heart that I could scarcely raise my countenance to . . . Heaven . . . if I tried to defraud [God] out of that [which is rightfully His]."⁵

This leads to a fifth reason to pay our tithes and offerings. We should pay them as a personal expression of love to a generous and merciful Father in Heaven. Through His grace God has dealt bread to the hungry and clothing to the poor. At various times in our lives that will include all of us, either temporally or spiritually speaking. For every one of us the gospel has broken forth as the light of the morning, driving back the darkness of ignorance and sorrow, fear and despair. In nation after nation His children have called and the Lord has answered. Through the movement of His gospel across the world, God is relieving the burdens of the weary and setting free those who are oppressed. His loving goodness has made our lives, rich or poor, near or far, "like a watered garden, . . . [from] a spring of water . . . [that faileth] not" (Isaiah 58:11; see also 58:6–10).

I express my deepest gratitude for every blessing of the gospel of Jesus Christ, especially that greatest of all gifts, the exemplary life and atoning death of God's Only Begotten Son. I know I can never repay heaven for any of this benevolence, but there are many ways I need to *try* to show my thankfulness.

One of those ways is in the payment of tithes and freewill offerings. I *want* to give something back, but I never want it to be (in King David's words) "that which doth cost me nothing" (2 Samuel 24:24).

I testify that the principle of tithing is of God, taught to us in such scriptural simplicity that we cannot doubt its divinity. May we all claim its blessings forever.

NOTES

From a talk given at general conference, October 2001.

1. Quoted by David B. Haight in Conference Report, April 1981, 57.
2. In *Ensign,* November 1996, 44.
2. In Conference Report, April 1900, 48.
3. In Conference Report, April 1968, 74.
4. *The Lord's Tenth,* pamphlet (Salt Lake City: The Church of Jesus Christ of Latter-day Saints, 1968), 10–11.

CHAPTER 14

"Let There Be Light"

O f all the plagues to strike our world in modern times, one of the most insidious is pornography. The cost, in human terms, is almost beyond calculation. In the face of this dark topic, I wish to consider how to eradicate it—with an increase of light.

What may be the most disturbing fact of all in a world as repulsive as the world of pornography is the reach of pornography into the lives of those least prepared to resist it—our children. As you know, reliable statistics accessing the online use of pornography are hard to come by, but a few years ago a Kaiser Family Foundation/NPR survey found that 31 percent of children aged ten to seventeen with computers at home had seen a pornographic Web site. In another study by the Kaiser Foundation, 70 percent of teens aged fifteen to seventeen said they had accidentally come across pornography on the Web. A survey revealed that, nationally, 5 percent of children between the ages of ten and seventeen using the Internet had received a solicitation for sex in the past year.[1]

Since these studies, now dated only by a few years, the problem has become worse. The number of homes with Internet access has increased dramatically, and cell phones and other technology popular with youth can now connect with the Web. Blogs, chat rooms, and community Web sites like Myspace.com have proliferated, along with the potential for contact with online sexual predators.

But of course we must always be vigilant to note that the problem is so much larger than this. As much as there is at least something of a national consensus on the evils of child pornography, there is, sadly, none whatever—yet—on pornography for and featuring adults. The scope and significance of the problem in the adult world is more pervasive than ever.

The simple fact of the matter is this: *Pornography victimizes everyone*—those who are addicted to it, those who live with them, a society that fosters it, a society that is trying to oppose it, even those who create it. It contaminates everyone.

Not long ago a Protestant periodical gave an account of a woman, now a believing, practicing Christian, who at one time acted in the kind of films that a generation ago were found only in back-alley movie theaters and are now openly sold in stores and shown on cable TV. She writes: "[Pornography is] one of the greatest deceptions of all time. Trust me, I know. I did it all the time, and I did it for the lust of power and the love of money. I never liked [men or] sex. . . . In fact I was more apt to spend time with Jack Daniels than [any other man of my choosing. Who wouldn't] hate being touched by strangers who care nothing about [you. Who wouldn't] hate being degraded. . . . Some women hate it so much you can hear them vomiting in the bathroom between scenes. . . . One of my friends went home after a long night of numbing her pain and put a pistol to her head and pulled the trigger. That was her way out.

"The truth is there is no fantasy in porn. It's all a lie. A closer look into the scenes of a porn star's life will show you a movie [that] industry doesn't want you to see. The real truth is [if] actresses want to end the shame and trauma of our lives [in that world] we can't do it alone. We need you . . . to fight for our freedom and give us back our honor. . . . We [need] you to throw out our movies and help [us] piece together the shattered fragments of our lives. We need you to pray for us . . . so God will hear and repair our ruined lives."[2]

Did you catch her references to money and power? The industry we're fighting is not about men or women or love or intimacy—it's about money, and the power money supposedly brings. The tragedy here is that the human soul is not a commodity of exchange, not a thing to be consumed and discarded, a thing one can buy for $19.99 plus tax and then, when tired or ashamed of it, throw in the trash bin.

The human soul is not a commodity of exchange, not a thing to be consumed and discarded.

And deep down everyone knows that, even those who are mired in the depths of this. One of our national associates in this fight wrote, "When I ask men who are sex addicts if they would want their wife or daughter to be in porn, 100 percent say, 'No.' . . . They want it to be somebody else's wife or daughter. They know this material is damaging [and the practice degrading.]"[3]

Years ago one of my personal heroes, President Spencer W. Kimball, made this observation:

"'We have witnessed the reduction of persons to things in a code number, a subscriber, a punched card. Each reduction indicates that the person is expendable, replaceable.' This renders men [and women as] functionaries and destroys their being and loses for them their self. . . . This is hauntingly true as people are 'used' to gratify physical passions in illegitimacy.

"We really do not 'love' things. We *use* things like doormats, automobiles, clothing, machines; but we love people by serving them and contributing to their permanent good."[4]

Of all the characteristics ascribed to Jesus Christ—whom the scriptures call the Light of the World—love is His most fundamental and most enduring virtue. We must remember that not only those who view pornography but also those who perform it are children of God, and furthermore are someone's son, someone's daughter here on earth as well. Despite all their sin we need to love them, serve them, save them if we can, and contribute to their permanent good. We can do that by following the pattern set by God at the outset of our earthly experience.

The book held sacred by Jews and Christians worldwide begins with these words:

"In the beginning God created the heaven and the earth. . . .

"And God said, Let there be light: and there was light.

"And God saw the light, that it was good: and God divided the light from the darkness" (Genesis 1:1, 3–4).

Our work is to divide the light from the darkness by lighting more and more candles. I can think of a few ways we could begin to do that.

First, let us be clear about the holder of the candles. I find it interesting that the first thing light reveals when a candle is lighted is the hand holding it. The Lord made this fascinating observation about personal light:

"The light of the body is the eye: therefore when thine eye is single, thy whole body also is full of light; but when thine eye is evil, thy body also is full of darkness.

"Take heed therefore that the light which is in thee be not darkness.

"If thy whole body therefore be full of light, having no part dark, the whole shall be full of light, as when the bright shining of a candle doth give thee light" (Luke 11:34–36).

The candles we hold up for others to see ought to be extensions of the light within ourselves. What we are shines more brightly than anything we say or do. If we are to fill the world with light, we must first face any tattered remnant of darkness that remains in our own souls.

What we are shines more brightly than anything we say or do. If we are to fill the world with light, we must first face any tattered remnant of darkness that remains in our own souls.

I invite you to join me in regularly turning inward to confront there *anything* we wouldn't want others to see. It may not be pornography, but it may be arrogance or unkindness, impatience or vanity, or any number of other flaws we need to remedy. Whatever it is let us trim our lamps, add oil, and make those changes necessary that allow us to hold up a brighter candle, a purer light. Christ focused some of His most pointed opprobrium for the hypocrite. We must *never* be guilty of that in this battle. Each of us must be the best person we can be in every way we can.

Second, let us educate ourselves. Light is not the absence of darkness; rather, darkness is the absence of light. Light and truth exist independently. This being the case, the more light we have, the more independent we are, and the freer we are to choose. With truth lighting the way, we are able to see and make choices we otherwise couldn't make.

Since we are agents with the ability to choose, the responsibility for our education rests first with us. Others may help—teachers, parents, leaders, friends, even those who are not friends but whose negative examples and misguided perspectives serve to instruct what not to do or what not to believe. Ultimately, however, the responsibility for getting the facts straight is ours. The work is ours. The choices are ours.

Keep in mind that any knowledge we gather can be both negative and positive. Yes, we will gather statistics and horror stories about the impact of the darkness on our society. But more important, we must also fill our hearts and minds with truth and light, with love and the Spirit of God. Too often we allow ourselves to be forced into a defensive, remedial position when we

Nothing is more constructive than a good, powerful, pure personal life.

could be more effective by taking positive, constructive action. And nothing is more constructive than a good, powerful, pure personal life.

Third, as we educate ourselves, we need to educate others. The promoters of darkness often seem to have direct access to the media microphone. We may not be able to take that away from them, but we can at least raise our own voices. We can teach correct principles often and in as many ways as possible.

Since darkness is the absence of light, surely the most powerful way to counter darkness is to fill the world with light. As Elder Robert D. Hales has observed: "Light and darkness cannot occupy the same space at the same time. Light dispels darkness. When light is present, darkness is vanquished and must depart. More importantly, darkness cannot conquer light unless the light is diminished or departs."[5]

Is it not part of our work as sons and daughters of God to encourage creative efforts that dispel darkness and replace it with light? How powerful a force for good would be a renaissance in literature, art, technology, and science that adds light rather than takes it away! Such a renaissance is possible. There are among us artists and artisans who need only to receive a little more support and encouragement from men and women of conscience to produce works that could rival those that half a millennium ago marked the end of Europe's Dark Age and the rise of a wonderful new cultural and spiritual Renaissance.

As we fill the earth with art (and media) that is good and uplifting—as we fill the earth with light and knowledge—our children will see the darkness for what it is. They will see that it is counterfeit, that it brings only sorrow, pain, and emptiness. They will come to prefer light and be attracted to that which is good and true.

Fourth, we can be vigilant. Some of the most effective work we can do, as was said about the Watergate scandal, is "follow the money." We can keep money out of the pockets of the merchants of immorality. Owners perspire when profits fail. We can work against the profitability of those who merchandise in human suffering and degradation. We can alert media moguls that we will ignore their services and the products they advertise as long as they remain in league with those who abuse the individual, undermine the structure of the family, and attack the moral fiber of society.

But again, if that is all we do, we have not filled the void with light. We must also support, encourage, and finance that which is positive and life-affirming: art and beauty—in short, truth—that encourages people to come out of the darkness into the light.

Lastly, as parents we must control use of the Internet in our own homes. We need to set and enforce family rules that protect us and our children from those who would sneak into our homes and there replace light with darkness. As citizens, we can seek controls on Internet use in public places. We can understand and teach others how to use the Internet safely. This wonderful tool is too valuable to all of us to let greedy individuals use it for their own selfish ends.

You are well aware of the Harry Potter books and movies by J. K. Rowling. One of the reasons the books are so popular, I think, is that they show children victorious in battle against dark forces. They give readers hope that, even in total darkness, there is that spark of light. Despite the powerful evil arrayed against them, they know they can defeat the darkness.

But fundamental to the message of the Harry Potter books is the idea that children don't—indeed, can't—fight their battles alone. In fact, the one gift that saves Harry over and over again is the love of his mother, who died protecting him from evil. Without any question one of those best "defenses against the dark arts"—to use a phrase from the Harry Potter books—is close family ties. Parental love, family activity, gentle teaching, and respectful conversation—sweet time together—can help keep the generations close and build bonds that will never be broken. A strong home and the love of parents is not infallible; we all know of children and teachers who give in to the darkness despite the best efforts of their loved ones. But both research and experience show that parental love and a happy home is the strongest defense our children have against anything the lords of darkness can throw at them.

Both research and experience show that parental love and a happy home is the strongest defense our children have against anything the lords of darkness can throw at them.

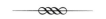

In this regard, recent findings bring good news: "The use of filters in families with teens has grown 65% in four years, from around 7 million users at the end of 2000, to close to 12 million today. Of all families in the United States connected to the Internet, 54% use Internet filters."[6]

These and similar statistics are encouraging. More parents are recognizing the need to protect their families. Most teens (73 percent) report that "their household computer is located in a public place inside the house," and most parents (64 percent) reported that they set rules about what their children do on the Internet. Unfortunately, 65 percent of all parents and 64 percent of all teens say that teens do things online that they "wouldn't want their parents to know about."[7]

We still have work to do.

The second greatest poet in the English language once wrote:

He that has light within his own clear breast
May sit i' the centre, and enjoy bright day:
But he that hides a dark soul and foul thoughts
Benighted walks under the mid-day sun;
Himself his own dungeon.[8]

Lighting candles can be a great adventure. Whatever else is revealed by the light, nothing becomes as clear as what we find in our own souls. May our journey into light be inspirational. And may the light you share show others the way to pure light, Eternal Light, God's light.

NOTES

From an address given at the Fourth Annual Guardian of the Light Dinner, May 3, 2006.

1. See The National Academy of Sciences, *Youth, Pornography, and the Internet*, 2002, 132–33.
2. Shelley Lubben, "The Truth Behind the Fantasy of Porn," Blazing Grace, http://www.blazingrace.org/thetruth.htm.
3. David Crary, quoting psychologist Mary Anne Layden, "Battle Brews As Porn Moves into Mainstream," Associated Press, Sunday, April 1, 2006, http://www.sfgate.com/cgi-bin/article.cgi?f=/n/a/2006/04/01/national/a131130S42.DTL
4. Spencer W. Kimball, *Faith Precedes the Miracle* (Salt Lake City: Deseret Book, 1972), 155–56; emphasis added.
5. Robert D. Hales, in Conference Report, April 2002, 80–81.
6. Amanda Lenhart, "Protecting Teens Online," *Pew Internet and American Life Project*, March 17, 2005, i.
7. "Protecting Teens Online," ii.
8. John Milton, *Comus*, lines 381–85.

CHAPTER 15

"All Things Are Possible to
Him That Believeth"

R eturning from the magnificent spiritual experience high
on the Mount of Transfiguration where He was
shrouded in glory and heard the voice of His Father say,
"This is my beloved son: hear him" (Mark 9:7), Jesus was under-
standably dismayed when He came upon a group of His disciples
and local scribes arguing and striving with one another in a hos-
tile way.

Responding to the Savior's inquiry as to the cause of this
contention, a man stepped forward, the father of an afflicted
child who said that the self-destructive spirit afflicting his son,
an infirmity the boy had since childhood, was getting increasingly more dangerous. Initially the father had approached Jesus'
disciples for a blessing, a cure of some kind, but they could not
provide it—apparently prompting the shouting match now in
full force. With the boy gnashing his teeth and foaming from
the mouth as he wallowed on the ground before them, the

father said to Jesus in something of a weary, last-resort tone of voice:

"If thou canst do any thing, have compassion on us, and help us.

"Jesus said unto him, If thou canst believe, all things are possible to him that believeth.

"And straightway the father of the child cried out, and said with tears, Lord, I believe; help thou mine unbelief" (Mark 9:14–24).

This is one of the greatest New Testament accounts we have probing the complexity of faith and the degrees one experiences in its development. The man's initial faith, by his own admission, is limited. But he has some faith. He did, after all, approach the disciples but, of course, met disappointment there. With whatever remaining faith he has, he turns to Jesus and says, "If *thou* canst *do* any thing," please help us, hoping perhaps Jesus might be able to succeed where all others have failed.

Christ, ever the teacher, seizes on the man's very language and limited faith and turns it back on him "If *thou* canst *believe*," Christ says, "all things are possible to him that believeth." In that very instant, in the length of time it takes to have that two-sentence exchange, this man's understanding begins to be enlightened. The look in the Savior's eye or the tone of His voice or the majesty of His bearing or simply the words He spoke—*something* touches this man spiritually and an inexorable change begins. Up to that moment he had thought that everything depended on others—doctors, soothsayers, priests, the disciples, or, here at the very last, Jesus. Only now, in this exchange, does he grasp that a great deal of the answer to his quest rests upon his own shoulders, or, more accurately, in his own soul.

So here, almost before our very eyes, we see a man address the issue of faith and we see the seed of faith begin to grow. "Straightaway" the scripture says, not slowly or skeptically or cynically but "straightaway" the father of the child cries out and sheds parental tears. After all, this is bone of his bone and flesh of his flesh. This is as close to home as it can get. This is a father pleading for his son. This is new faith versus old fear in a fist-fight, a fear perhaps only parents of struggling children can ever know. He cries, literally, "Lord, I believe; help thou mine unbelief." And of course we know the miraculous blessing that then comes as a result of such an honest, earnest assertion.

May I suggest several possible lessons embedded in this tender scriptural text.

First let me note in this painful, personal drama that the father asserts his strength first, and only then acknowledges his lack. His initial declaration is affirmative, unwavering, even inspiring. In wanting to meet his responsibility in this matter he declares what faith he has—apparently without hesitation: "Lord, I believe!"

I would ask all of us, in moments of fear or doubt or troubling times, to hold the ground we have already won even if that ground is limited and under attack. In the course of life, problems are going to come, questions are going to arise, some spiritual equivalent of this foaming and gnashing loved one is going to face us. Remember, it wasn't just "trouble" Hamlet felt he had to fight, it was a "sea of troubles."[1] That is the way life goes sometimes. In fact, that is one of the purposes of life.

When you are confronted with challenges that are difficult to conquer or have questions arise, the answers to which you do not know, *hold fast to the things you do know*. Hang on to your firmest foundation, however limited that may be, and from that position of strength face the unknown. When questions of history or science or philosophy arise, when sorrow or disappointment or despair seem to stalk you, do what this father did—assert all the faith you *do* have, and everybody has some! If we can do just that much we will learn the truthfulness of Jesus' promise—that even mustard-seed-sized faith will ultimately move any mountain. "All things are possible to him that believeth."

When you are confronted with challenges that are difficult to conquer or have questions arise, the answers to which you do not know, hold fast to the things you do know.

The converse of this counsel to you obviously follows. When the pressure is on, when crunch time hits, don't make your first declaration one of unbelief. That is the wrong end of the lance with which to approach a problem. Someone has said, "The first rule of holes is, when you are in one, stop digging." Surely the first rule of fueling faith is not to start by saying how much of it you *don't* have. You've got more than you think, and if you will assert that first, limited as it is, the miracle of it will lead you on, step by step, across your void of mystery or dread. If you will do this, Jesus will take *you* by the hand, just as He did this afflicted young man in the story, and *you* will be "lifted up," you will "arise" in the timetable of the Lord—to health and happiness and brighter days ahead, all the brighter because your faith has been increased in the process.

Second, may I say that this father's faith is not the only faith being probed and prodded here. It is the faith of the entire audience, then and now, the whole field of onlookers—the disciples who could not provide a miracle because their faith (and in this case their fasting) was insufficient, the scribes who were so delighted to jeer the disciples' failure, the entire multitude who were shouting about and exploiting the situation toward no end at all.

It is to the whole audience, to every one of them, to every one of *us* that Jesus says in some disappointment, "O faithless generation, how long shall I suffer you?" (Mark 9:19).

It is not just to this frantic father, it is to you and me and every other living soul that Christ says, "If thou canst believe, all things are possible to him that believeth." In this broader application of the scripture, wouldn't it be interesting to know if the father in this story had you and me in mind, as well as his son and himself, when he said to Jesus (notice the pronoun): "Have compassion on *us*, help *us*." In any case, he knew it wasn't only his child who needed help, he needed it too. And we do as well. Yes, unfortunately, men and women in all ages, including our own, stand condemned under the indictment, "O faithless generation." In at least some aspects of our life, you and I, even believers that we are, need to be more willing to humble ourselves, to bow our heads, and to lower our voices, saying, "Lord, help thou mine unbelief."

Let us constantly, repeatedly affirm our belief, even as we wrestle with unbelief.

Any weakness, any uncertainty, any wavering—that will *never* be in God. Take my word for it. We do not need to waste any breath inquiring haltingly of Him, "If thou canst do any thing . . ." Trust me, or rather trust Him—He can not only do anything, he can do *everything.* No, the challenge is always with us. As one scholar said in a different context, "When the infinite fullness is poured forth, it is not the oil's fault if there is loss. It will only be the fault of the vessels that fail to contain it."[2]

I testify to you that God, "the Infinite Fullness" as mentioned here, will not fail us. I pray that we will not fail Him. I testify of His love, His mercy, His compassion and forgiveness. He *wants* to bless us, far more than our limited minds or experience can comprehend, and He wants us to keep His commandments. Let us constantly, repeatedly affirm our belief, even as we wrestle with unbelief. And let us be the very best living examples of our religion's virtues and values as we try to do so. "All things are possible to him that believeth."

NOTES

From an address given at Chapman University, April 26, 2005.

1. William Shakespeare, *Hamlet,* act III, scene i.
2. Frederic W. Farrar, *The Life of Christ* (New York: E. P. Dutton and Company, 1883).

TRUE PROPHETS AND TRUE PRINCIPLES

CHAPTER 16

THE RESTORATION

The purpose of mortality, outlined from before the foundation of the world, is summarized in Heavenly Father's sending His spirit children to earth to gain bodies, learn the lessons of our second estate, and embrace the gospel of Jesus Christ. To guide us in that journey and to do everything possible toward the successful realization of it, He has repeatedly, from the beginning, sent angels from on high and put prophets on the earth to teach us, to help us, to warn us, and to bless us.

Alma taught: "And after God had appointed . . . these things, . . . he saw that it was expedient that man should know concerning the things whereof he had appointed unto them;

"Therefore he sent angels to converse with them, . . .

"And [men] began from that time forth to call on his name; therefore God conversed with men [sometimes personally, but more regularly through his anointed prophets], and made known unto them the plan of redemption, which had been prepared from the foundation of the world; and this he made known unto them according to their faith and repentance and their holy works" (Alma 12:28–30).

And so it goes—or so it was *supposed* to go. The problem is that there was another force, a dark and malicious force, in this equation, and he was determined (is still determined!) that there would be no faith and repentance and holy works, at least not if he could do anything about it. And sometimes he succeeded. In fact, across most of the world, for most of the time, with most of the people, he succeeded tragically well. Prophets were rejected or stoned or killed, faithful people (few as they were in some cases) were abused and tormented by the ungodly, and the angels wept, having to be restrained from sweeping down to cleanse the earth from the willful acts of men and their rejection of the gospel of Jesus Christ.

And it wasn't just angels who wept. One of the most plaintive scriptures in all of holy writ records: And Enoch beheld that "the power of Satan was upon all the face of the earth. . . .

" . . . And he had a great chain in his hand, and it veiled the whole face of the earth with darkness; and he looked up and laughed, and his angels rejoiced. . . .

"And it came to pass that the God of heaven looked upon the residue of the people, and he wept; and Enoch bore record of it, saying: How is it that the heavens weep, and shed forth their tears as the rain upon the mountains? . . .

"The Lord said unto Enoch: Behold these thy brethren; they are the workmanship of mine own hands, and I gave unto them their knowledge, in the day I created them; and in the Garden of Eden, gave I unto man his agency;

"And unto thy brethren have I . . . given commandment, that they should love one another, and that they should choose me, their Father; but behold, they are without affection, and they hate their own blood; . . .

" . . . Misery shall be their doom; and the whole heavens shall weep over them, even all the workmanship of mine hands; wherefore should not the heavens weep, seeing these shall suffer? . . .

"And [the Lord] . . . told Enoch all the doings of the children of men; wherefore Enoch knew, and looked upon their wickedness, and their misery, and wept and stretched forth his arms, and his heart swelled wide as eternity; and his bowels yearned; and all eternity shook" (Moses 7:24, 26, 28, 32–33, 37, 41).

That paints the scriptural picture of the dispensations: the power of goodness, God in His heaven and prophets on the earth, laboring in a combined effort to save the souls of the children of men. And in opposition there was the reality of evil, the sinfulness of Satan and his minions, spreading untruths and misery, pain and despair, prompting sorrow in heaven and heartache on earth.

That was the experience for Adam and his family, caught in this battle almost the moment they left the Garden of Eden (figuratively speaking). And we have just read that it was still the same in Enoch's day. It was so leading up to Noah's time and the total cleansing of the earth required then. It was the same in Abraham's day, in Moses' day, in Isaiah's and Jeremiah's and Ezekiel's day. In short, it was the same experience, more or less, in every age—down through the record of time in the Old World, and then with the Jaredites and Father Lehi's descendants it was the same in the New World as well.

All of this tension, this constant movement between revelation and rejection, between prophets and apostasy, was captured in a parable by Jesus, the very Son of God Himself. Near the end of His mortal ministry He said by way of both history and prophecy:

"Hear another parable: There was a certain householder, which planted a vineyard, and hedged it round about, and digged a winepress in it, and built a tower, and let it out to husbandmen, and went into a far country:

"And when the time of the fruit drew near, he sent his servants to the husbandmen, that they might receive the fruits of it.

"And the husbandmen took his servants, and beat one, and killed another, and stoned another.

"Again, he sent other servants more than the first: and they did unto them likewise.

"But last of all he sent unto them his son, saying, They will reverence my son.

"But when the husbandmen saw the son, they said among themselves, This is the heir; come, let us kill him, and let us seize on his inheritance.

"And they caught him, and cast him out of the vineyard, and slew him.

"When the lord therefore of the vineyard cometh, what will he do unto those husbandmen?

"They say unto him, He will miserably destroy those wicked men, and will let out his vineyard unto other husbandmen, which shall render him the fruits in their seasons" (Matthew 21:33–41).

That brief parable summarizes the experience of revelation and apostasy as it has been repeated prophet after prophet and dispensation after dispensation. Of course, Jesus gave that parable knowing the cycle would continue, even to the point that

His life would be taken and another long night of apostasy would follow.

For those first decades following Jesus' death the Apostles were able to keep the doctrines pure, but as they died or were killed without passing on their ordinations and without the revelation they had received, truly the vineyard of the Lord was plundered. Eventually priesthood keys and presiding priesthood authority were taken from the earth. Doctrines were corrupted and unauthorized changes were made in Church ordinances and Church organization. Scholasticism replaced inspiration, philosophy obscured what had been simple truths, and false ideas crept in everywhere. Much of the knowledge of the true character and nature of God the Father, His Son Jesus Christ, and the Holy Ghost was lost. The doctrines of faith, repentance, baptism, and the gift of the Holy Ghost became distorted or abused or forgotten. The principle of revelation was denied, and the canon of scripture was declared to be closed. The role of prophets and Apostles as had been known in those earlier dispensations ceased. No such men were found upon the earth.

To put my own adaptation on what a British scholar not of our faith has said about that era, the worship of the members in the days of the Apostles was plain and precious, without excess and without images; but as false ideas entered and prevailed, ancient simplicity disappeared. The common meal, in which the early

> *The worship of the members in the days of the Apostles was plain and precious, without excess and without images; but as false ideas entered and prevailed, ancient simplicity disappeared.*

Christians used symbols of bread and wine to commemorate their Savior's Last Supper, gradually became an erroneous doctrine of transubstantiation; the table at which they sat to partake turned into an altar of exclusivity and adornment; the church membership that Christ designed to be one body was divided into sacerdotal clergy and nonparticipating laity. When the power of prophesying was lost, and the spiritual gifts promised to the congregation were claimed by a restricted order of ministers alone, those priests moved ever further from the common people. The simple expressions of gospel love prompted by the Holy Spirit (and therefore powerful enough to break in pieces the stony heart while binding up the broken one) were replaced by convoluted creeds and scholarly lectures.[1]

As someone lamented, once there had been wooden chalices and golden priests; later there were only golden chalices and wooden priests.

After centuries of spiritual darkness, truth-seeking men and women protested against such erroneous religious practices. They recognized that many of the doctrines and ordinances of the gospel had been changed or lost. They sought for greater spiritual light, and many spoke of the need for a restoration of truth. Gradually the great Protestant Reformation began in Europe, with legendary names like Luther, Calvin, and Zwingli leading the way. That tide rolled on to England, where the Reformation gathered such momentum that Henry VIII, for rather selfish purposes, was able to make a formal break with papal authority and Europe's centuries-long tie to the church in Rome.

But the real voice of freedom and the grand setting not for a reformation but a *restoration* came on this continent following the settling of the Pilgrims and Puritans, those early seekers who were determined to find a better and a holier way.

God was working on the minds of many to make the circumstances right for a final restoration of the gospel, for one last effort to do even more completely, and more finally, that which had been done down through the ages— the calling of prophets, the appearing of angels, the reality of righteousness coming down from heaven and truth springing forth out of the earth (see Moses 7:62).

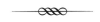

God was working on the minds of many to make the circumstances right for a final restoration of the gospel.

Ours is the message of that Restoration: that the Father and the Son appeared to the fourteen-year-old Joseph Smith in the spring of 1820 in a New York woodland grove now called sacred because of the divinity that was manifest there.

That event signaled the beginning of the last and greatest of all gospel dispensations, a dispensation that would be the setting for and the vehicle of the Restoration of the gospel of Jesus Christ in all its glory, with priesthood keys, priesthood authority, saving principles, and saving ordinances. All were restored from those earlier dispensations, when good men, true prophets, and living Apostles had tried but had ultimately been rebuffed—or killed—in their effort to make eternal truths efficacious for all mankind.

You know the story well. You must "open your mouth" to share it at every opportunity (see D&C 28:16). It is central to our message. Confused by what he called a "war of words" and a "tumult of opinions" among the contesting religious parties in his community, some crying "lo, here" and others "lo, there," the boy Joseph said it was impossible for a person young as he was to know who was right and who was wrong in a search for true religion (see Joseph Smith—History 1:5–10).

So, trusting in the promise of the first chapter of James, a verse of scripture destined to change the history of the world, Joseph went into the woods near his family home to offer his first vocal prayer to God. No sooner had he begun that prayer than thick darkness gathered around him, a force so powerful from an enemy so real that he feared he would be destroyed in both body and soul (see Joseph Smith—History 1:11–15).

Exerting all his power to call upon God for deliverance, he said, "at this moment of great alarm, I saw a pillar of light exactly over my head, above the brightness of the sun, which descended gradually until it fell upon me. It no sooner appeared than I found myself delivered from the enemy which held me bound. When the light rested upon me I saw two Personages, whose brightness and glory defy all description, standing above me in the air. One of them spake unto me, calling me by name and said, pointing to the other—*This is My Beloved Son. Hear Him!*" (Joseph Smith—History 1:16–17; emphasis in original).

The rest is, as we say, history—sacred history. For the first time in nearly 1,800 years the heavens had been divinely rent. God had once again called a prophet—young, in the tradition of Samuel and David, Nephi and Mormon—and revelation again flowed from the fountain of the Most High.

Moroni came next with an ancient record containing the fulness of the gospel. He was followed by John the Baptist, who came with Aaronic Priesthood keys to entertain angels and baptize for the remission of sins. Within weeks of that event, Peter, James, and John appeared to confer the priesthood of

Melchizedek, including the holy Apostleship. Other prophets came to confer sacred keys and to teach the boy prophet.

Revelation flowed from heaven monthly, weekly, almost daily it seemed, relative to the organization of the Church and the doctrines of the kingdom of God. As one of my mission-president friends describes it, "Never in earth's history had so many marvelous and miraculous things happened in so short a time."[2] Truly these were "days never to be forgotten" (Joseph Smith—History 1:71, footnote). And it is not by coincidence that the LDS hymnal begins with this anthem to the Restoration:

> *The morning breaks, the shadows flee;*
> *Lo, Zion's standard is unfurled!*
> *The dawning of a brighter day, . . .*
> *Majestic rises on the world.*[3]

What a glorious moment in the annals of time, and we have been born to help unfurl that standard and see its splendor carried to all the nations of the earth.

That is why ours is such a sacred trust. We are those latter-day "other" husbandmen of whom the Savior spoke in that parable, husbandmen to whom God would give latter-day stewardship over His harvest. We are they who, when so much had been wrong and cruel and sinful down through time, would be instruments in the hand of God for making it right, for bringing the light of the restored gospel and the love of the Lord to the dark and troubled minds of men. It is *we* who are called to be among those "first laborers in this last kingdom" (D&C 88:74), to work valiantly in a field that is white, all ready to harvest, thrusting in our sickle with our might, and rendering unto Him the fruits of our labor (see D&C 4:4; Matthew 21:41).

Of his assignment in life Hamlet lamented, "The time is out of joint: O cursed spite, / That ever I was born to set it right."[4]

We are they who, when so much had been wrong and cruel and sinful down through time, would be instruments in the hand of God for making it right.

Not us! No such dreariness from the Saints in our day! No, ours is a "dream job"—at least ancient prophets and Apostles did dream of us and the day in which we would be privileged to live.

The Prophet Joseph Smith said, "The building up of Zion is a cause that has interested the people of God in every age; it is a theme upon which prophets, priests, and kings have dwelt with peculiar delight; *they have looked forward with joyful anticipation to the day in which we live;* and fired with heavenly and joyful anticipations *they have sung and written and prophesied of this our day;* . . . we are the favored people that God has [chosen] to bring about the Latter-day glory."[5]

The charge we have been given is plain and emphatic regarding the message we are to declare to the world. We are told that God spoke to Joseph Smith from heaven and gave him commandments and that those commandments were in turn to be announced to all the children of men. One last time the words of the living God were to be heralded again among men as they had been anciently, only this time more completely, more universally, and more successfully. The significance of such a moment in history is breathtaking.

In one such revelation the Lord said, "Thou shalt preach the fulness of my gospel, which I have sent forth in these last days, the covenant which I have sent forth to recover my people, which are of the house of Israel" (D&C 39:11).

Yet another time He said, "I call upon the weak things of the world, those who are unlearned and despised, to thrash the nations by the power of my Spirit;

"And their arm shall be my arm, and I will be their shield and their buckler; and I will gird up their loins, and they shall fight manfully for me; and their enemies shall be under their feet; and I will let fall the sword in their behalf, and by the fire of mine indignation will I preserve them" (D&C 35:13–14).

We are those "weak things of the world," the "unlearned and despised," at least in the eyes of some. So be it. So, too, were the ancients described. Just remember that by the mouth of God's own witness it is "the weak things of the world [that] shall come forth and break down the mighty and strong ones" (D&C 1:19), so "fight manfully" in this cause (see D&C 35:14).

To be successful, to be powerful in the hands of the Lord, I ask you to remember three things, focusing on the Restoration.

First, I ask you to remember this oft-told but too frequently forgotten story of President David O. McKay's father, who served a mission to Scotland in the 1880s. In President McKay's own words he said:

"When [my father] began preaching in his native land and bore testimony of the restoration of the gospel of Jesus Christ, he noticed that the people turned away from him. They were bitter in their hearts against anything Mormon, and the name of Joseph Smith seemed to arouse antagonism in their hearts. One day he concluded that the best way to reach these people would be to preach just . . . simple principles, . . . and not bear testimony of the restoration. In a month or so he became oppressed with a gloomy, downcast feeling and he could not enter into the spirit of his work. He did not really know what was the matter, but his mind became obstructed; his spirit became depressed; he was oppressed and hampered; and that feeling of depression continued until it weighed him down with such heaviness that he went to the Lord and said, 'Unless I can get this feeling removed, I shall have to go home. I can't continue having my work thus hampered.'

"The discouragement continued for some time after that, when, one morning before daylight, following a sleepless night, he decided to retire to a cave, . . . where he knew he would be shut off from the world entirely, and there pour out his soul to God and ask why he was oppressed with this feeling, what he had done, and what he could do to throw it off and continue his work. He started out in the dark toward the cave. He became so eager to get to it that he started to run. As he was leaving the town, he was hailed by an officer who wanted to know what was the matter. He gave some noncommittal but satisfactory reply and was permitted to go on. Something just seemed to drive him; he had to get relief. He entered the . . . sheltered opening, and said, 'Oh, Father, what can I do to have this feeling removed? I must have it lifted or I cannot continue in this work'; and he heard a voice, as distinct as the tone I am now uttering, say: 'Testify that Joseph Smith is a prophet of God.' Remembering then what he . . . had decided six weeks . . . before, and becoming overwhelmed with the thought [that] he had not given [Joseph Smith's] special mission the attention it deserved, . . . he cried in his heart, 'Lord, it is enough,' and went out from the cave.

" . . . As a boy, I sat and heard that testimony," President

McKay said, "from one whom I treasured and honored as . . . I treasured no other man in the world, and that assurance [regarding Joseph Smith and the Restoration] was instilled in my youthful soul."[6]

Second, *you* must be your first convert regarding this great message of the restored gospel. Everything you will want for the people with whom you share the gospel, Heavenly Father wants for you. You will want them to pray more earnestly; He wants you to pray more earnestly. You will want them to study more deeply; He wants you to study more deeply. You will want them to repent sincerely; He wants you to repent sincerely. You will want a "mighty change" in their hearts; He wants a mighty change in your heart (see Mosiah 5:2). Above all, you will want them to feel His Spirit and obey it; well, above all He will want you to feel His Spirit and obey it. Remember this truth: *Everything in the conversion process must happen to you before it can happen to them—everything.*

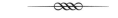

Everything you will want for the people with whom you share the gospel, Heavenly Father wants for you.

To paraphrase just slightly something President Harold B. Lee said once, the measure of your personal conversion and whether or not you hold fast to the ideals of the Church will depend in great measure on your conviction that Joseph Smith was a true prophet of God, a foreordained instrument in the hand of heaven for the restoration of the gospel of Jesus Christ, and that that testimony has burned down into your heart like fire.[7]

Third, you must have a personal testimony of those whom

Joseph said he saw. And I testify that he did see them. You must have your own unwavering conviction that God is our Father, the author of eternity's loving plan, the literal Father of Jesus Christ, and *our* Father—the Father of our spirits. You must know with utmost conviction that He lives and loves us forever.

You must also know in the deepest recesses of your heart that to show that love and to save us, His children, He sent His

Your love for Jesus Christ and your discipleship in His cause must be the consuming preoccupation and passion of your mortality.

perfect Son—His Firstborn in the spirit world and His Only Begotten here on earth—to fulfill heaven's divine plan, to become the Savior and Redeemer of the world. *Your love for Jesus Christ and your discipleship in His cause must be the consuming preoccupation and passion of your mortality.* You must strive every day to know the Savior in the most personal way that you can—to study His life, to learn His teachings, to follow His doctrine, to reverence His priesthood.

I testify to you that Jesus is the Holy Messiah, the Promised One, the Beginning and the End. I testify with King Benjamin that there never shall be any "other name given nor any other way nor means whereby salvation can come unto the children of men, [except] in and through the name of Christ, the Lord Omnipotent" (Mosiah 3:17; see also Acts 4:12).

And you must carry in your heart forever the deepest possible gratitude for His merciful Atonement and the joy of the Resurrection it purchased.

The heart of the gospel message is that with a complete

offering of His body, His blood, and the anguish of His spirit, Christ atoned for the initial transgression of Adam and Eve in the Garden of Eden and also for the personal sins of everyone else who would ever live in this world until the end of time. The Atonement of Christ, which makes our return to the Father possible, is rightfully seen as the central fact, the crucial foundation, the chief doctrine of the great and eternal plan of happiness.

I testify that He is our Savior, the Bishop and Shepherd of our souls, the Bright and Morning Star (see 1 Peter 2:25; Revelation 22:16). I know that our garments can be washed white only in the blood of that Lamb, slain from the foundation of the world (see Revelation 13:8; Moses 7:47). I testify that He was the great High Priest, the chief cornerstone of His Church in the meridian of time (see Hebrews 4:14; Ephesians 2:20). And is so in this last and greatest of all dispensations.

I testify that He lives, that the whole triumph of the gospel is that He lives. And because He does, so will we.

NOTES

From an address given at a seminar to new mission presidents, June 21, 2005.

1. See Edward Backhouse, *Early Church History to the Death of Constantine,* ed. Charles Tylor (London, 1884), 417–18; quoted in Joseph Fielding McConkie, *Here We Stand* (Salt Lake City: Deseret Book, 1995), 22–23.
2. McConkie, *Here We Stand,* 59.
3. "The Morning Breaks," *Hymns of The Church of Jesus Christ of Latter-day Saints* (Salt Lake City: The Church of Jesus Christ of Latter-day Saints, 1985), no. 1.
4. William Shakespeare, *Hamlet,* act I, scene v.
5. Joseph Smith, *History of The Church of Jesus Christ of Latter-day Saints,* 7 vols. (Salt Lake City: The Church of Jesus Christ of Latter-day Saints, 1932–1952), 4:607–10; emphasis added.

6. *Cherished Experiences from the Writings of President David O. McKay,* comp. Clare Middlemiss, rev. ed. (Salt Lake City: Deseret Book, 1976), 11–12.

7. See *The Teachings of Harold B. Lee,* ed. Clyde J. Williams (Salt Lake City: Bookcraft, 1996), 520.

CHAPTER 17

PROPHETS, SEERS, AND REVELATORS

In this chapter I wish to address something of the Apostleship and the importance of its perpetuation in the true Church of Jesus Christ. In so doing I refer not to the men who hold that office but rather to the office itself, a calling in the holy Melchizedek Priesthood that the Savior Himself has designated for the watchcare of His people and the witnessing of His name.

In order to establish a church that would continue under His direction even after He was taken from the earth, Jesus "went . . . into a mountain to pray, and continued all night in prayer to God.

"And when it was day, he called unto him his disciples: and of them he chose twelve, whom also he named apostles" (Luke 6:12–13).

Later on, Paul would teach that the Savior, knowing the inevitability of His death, had done this to give the Church a "foundation of . . . apostles and prophets" (Ephesians 2:20).

These brethren and the other officers of the Church would serve under the direction of the resurrected Christ.

Why? Among other reasons, so "that we henceforth be no more children, tossed to and fro, and carried about with every wind of doctrine, by the sleight of men, and cunning craftiness, whereby they lie in wait to deceive" (Ephesians 4:14).

Thus the apostolic and prophetic foundation of the Church was to bless in all times, but *especially* in times of adversity or danger, times when we might feel like children, confused or disoriented, perhaps a little fearful, times in which the devious hand of men or the maliciousness of the devil would attempt to unsettle or mislead. Against such times as come in our modern day, the First Presidency and Quorum of the Twelve are commissioned by God and sustained by you as "prophets, seers, and revelators," with the President of the Church sustained as *the* prophet, seer, and revelator, the *senior* Apostle, and as such the only man authorized to exercise all of the revelatory and administrative keys for the Church.

The apostolic and prophetic foundation of the Church was to bless in all times, but especially *in times of adversity or danger.*

In New Testament times, in Book of Mormon times, and in modern times these officers form the foundation stones of the true Church, positioned around and gaining their strength from the chief cornerstone, "the rock of our Redeemer, who is [Jesus] Christ, the Son of God" (Helaman 5:12), He who is the great "Apostle and High Priest of our profession," to use Paul's phrase (Hebrews 3:1). Such a foundation in Christ was and is always to be a protection in days "when the devil shall send forth his mighty winds, yea, his shafts in the whirlwind, yea, when all his hail and his mighty storm shall beat upon you." In such days as we are now in—and will more or less always be in—the storms of life "shall have no power over you . . . because of the rock upon which ye are built, which is a sure foundation, a foundation whereon if men build they cannot fall" (Helaman 5:12).

I once attended a stake conference in the lovely little mountain community of Prescott, Arizona. Following the delightful events of that weekend a sister silently slipped me a note as she and others came by to shake hands and say good-bye. With some hesitation I share a portion of it with you here. Please focus on the doctrine this sister teaches, not the participants in the exchange.

"Dear Elder Holland, thank you for the testimony you bore in this conference of the Savior and His love. Forty-one years ago I prayed earnestly to the Lord and told Him I wished I had lived on earth when the Apostles walked upon it, when there had been a true Church, and when Christ's voice was still heard. Within a year of that prayer Heavenly Father sent two LDS missionaries to me, and I found that all those hopes could be realized. Perhaps some hour when you are tired or troubled, this note will help you remember why hearing your voice and shaking your hand is so important to me and to millions just like me. Your sister in love and gratitude, Gloria Clements."

Well, Sister Clements, your very tender note recalled for me a similar hope and almost the same language once used in my own family. In the tumultuous years of the first settlements in this nation, Roger Williams, my volatile and determined tenth great-grandfather, fled—not entirely of his own volition—from the Massachusetts Bay Colony and settled in what is now the state of Rhode Island. He called his headquarters Providence, the very name itself revealing his lifelong quest for divine interventions and heavenly manifestations. But he never found what he felt was the true New Testament church of earlier times. Of this disappointed seeker the legendary Cotton Mather said, "Mr. Williams [finally] told [his followers] 'that being himself misled, he had [misled them,' and] he was now satisfied that there was none upon earth that could administer baptism [or any of the ordinances of the gospel], . . . [so] he advised them therefore to *forego* all . . . and wait for the coming of new apostles."[1] Roger Williams did not live to see those longed-for new Apostles raised up, but in a future time I hope to be able to tell him personally that his posterity did live to see such.

Anxiety and expectation regarding the need for divine direction was not uncommon among those religious reformers who set the stage for the Restoration of the gospel. One of the most famous of the New England preachers, Jonathan Edwards, said, "It seems to me a[n] . . . unreasonable thing, to suppose that there should be a God . . . that has so much concern [for us], . . . and yet that he should never speak, . . . that there should be no word [from him]."[2]

"It is the office of a true teacher to show us that God is, not was; that He speaketh, not spake." (Ralph Waldo Emerson)

Later, the incomparable Ralph Waldo Emerson rocked the very foundations of New England ecclesiastical orthodoxy when he said to the Divinity School at Harvard: "It is my duty to say to you that the need was never greater [for] new revelation than now. . . . The doctrine of inspiration is lost. . . . Miracles, prophecy, . . . the holy life, exist as ancient history [only]. . . .

166

Men have come to speak of . . . revelation as somewhat long ago given and done, as if God were dead. . . . It is the office of a true teacher," he warned, "to show us that God is, not was; that He speaketh, not spake."[3] In essence, Mr. Emerson was saying, "If you persist in handing out stones when people ask for bread, they will eventually stop coming to the bakery."[4]

Consider these stunning indictments from the towering figures of American history, to say nothing of the prayers of a Gloria Clements, and it highlights in bold relief the powerful message of The Church of Jesus Christ of Latter-day Saints, especially to those who meet our missionaries. Prophets? Seers? Revelators? The events of 1820 and 1830, and the events of nearly two centuries that have followed, declare that revelations and those who receive them are not "long ago given and done."

In the very year Mr. Emerson gave his Divinity School address implicitly pleading for such, Elder John Taylor, a young English immigrant to this country, was called to be an Apostle of the Lord Jesus Christ, a prophet, seer, and revelator. In that calling Elder Taylor once said in sympathy with honest seekers of truth: "Whoever heard of true religion without communication with God? To me the thing is the most absurd that the human mind could conceive of. I do not wonder," said Brother Taylor, "[that] when the people generally reject the principle of present revelation, skepticism and infidelity prevail to such an alarming extent. I do not wonder," he continued, "that so many men treat religion with contempt, and regard it as something not worth the attention of intelligent beings, for without revelation religion is a mockery and a farce. . . . *The principle of present revelation . . . is the very foundation of our religion.*"[5]

The principle of present revelation? The very foundation of our religion? Let me return from those foundations to the

167

present, the here and now, the twenty-first century. For one and all—ecclesiastics, historians, and laymen alike—the issue is still the same. Are the heavens open? Does God reveal His will to prophets and Apostles as in days of old? That they are and that He does is the unflinching declaration of The Church of Jesus Christ of Latter-day Saints to all the world. And in that declaration lies the significance of Joseph Smith, the Prophet, for nearly 200 years now.

His life asked and answered the question "Do you believe God speaks to man?" In all else that he accomplished in his brief thirty-eight and a half years, Joseph left us above all else the resolute legacy of divine revelation—not a single, isolated revelation without evidence or consequence, and not "a mild sort of inspiration seeping into the minds of all good people" everywhere, but specific, documented, ongoing directions from God. As a good friend and faithful LDS scholar has succinctly put it, "At a time when the origins of Christianity were under assault by the forces of Enlightenment rationality, Joseph Smith [unequivocally and singlehandedly] returned modern Christianity to its origins in revelation."[6]

In all else that he accomplished . . . Joseph left us above all else the resolute legacy of divine revelation.

We do "thank thee, O God, for a prophet to guide us in these latter days,"[7] because many of those days will be windblown and tempest-tossed. We give thanks for that morning in the spring of 1820 when the Father and the Son appeared in glory to a fourteen-year-old boy. We give thanks for that morning when Peter, James, and John came to restore the keys of the holy priesthood and all the offices in it. And so it goes down to a day such as this, and so it will go continually until the Savior comes.

In a world of unrest and fear, political turmoil and moral drift, I testify that Jesus is the Christ—that He is the living Bread and living Water—still, yet, and always the great Shield of safety in our lives, the mighty Stone of Israel, the Anchor of this His living Church. I testify of His prophets, seers, and revelators, who constitute the ongoing foundation of that Church and bear witness that such offices and such oracles are at work now, under the guidance of the Savior of us all, in and for our very needful day.

NOTES

From a talk given at general conference, October 2004.

1. *Magnalia Christi Americana* (1853), 2:498.
2. *The Works of Jonathan Edwards*, vol. 18, *The "Miscellanies," 501–832*, ed. Ava Chamberlain (New Haven: Yale University Press, 2000), 89–90.
3. *The Complete Essays and Other Writings of Ralph Waldo Emerson*, ed. Brooks Atkinson (New York: The Modern Library, 1940), 75, 71, 80.
4. Louis Cassels, quoted in Howard W. Hunter, "Spiritual Famine," *Ensign,* January 1973, 64.
5. "Discourse by John Taylor," *Deseret News,* 4 March 1874, 68; emphasis added.
6. See Richard L. Bushman's essay "A Joseph Smith for the Twenty-First Century" in *Believing History* (New York: Columbia University Press, 2004). These citations are from page 274, but the essay should be read in its entirety.
7. "We Thank Thee, O God, for a Prophet," *Hymns of The Church of Jesus Christ of Latter-day Saints* (Salt Lake City: The Church of Jesus Christ of Latter-day Saints, 1985), no. 19.

CHAPTER 18

PROPHETS IN THE LAND AGAIN

Not long after our friend Carolyn Rasmus joined the faculty of Brigham Young University, a group of her new teaching colleagues invited her to join them on a Saturday hike in the mountains above Provo. Carolyn was not a member of The Church of Jesus Christ of Latter-day Saints, but she had felt particularly welcome in her new circle of associates. She eagerly joined them for the climb.

As the sun steadily rose, so did the hikers on the mountainside. Then, as the ten o'clock hour approached, the group began to find places to sit down. Carolyn thought, "This is wonderful. How did they know I needed the rest?" and she, too, looked for a comfortable spot to stretch out. But the participants seemed unusually earnest about this particular break, some pulling out pencils and notebooks while one intently dialed a transistor radio.

What then happened would be a turning point in her life

forever. One of her friends said, "Carolyn, we need to explain something. This is the first Saturday in October, and for us that means not only lovely weather and bright fall foliage, but it also means a general conference of the Church. As Latter-day Saints, wherever we are or whatever we are doing, we stop and listen. So we are going to sit here among the oak and the pines, look out over the valley below, and listen to the prophets of God for a couple of hours."

"A couple of hours!" thought Carolyn. "I didn't know there were prophets of God still living," she said, "and I certainly didn't know there were two hours' worth!" Little did she know that they were going to stop again at two o'clock that afternoon for another two hours and then invite her to tune in at home for four more the next day.

Well, the rest is history. With the gift of a leather-bound copy of the scriptures from her students, the love of friends and families in the LDS ward she began to attend, and spiritual experiences we want all who make their way into the light of the gospel to have, Carolyn was baptized and confirmed a member of the Church. The rest is, as they say, history. With her introduction to general conference that day sitting high atop Y Mountain, Sister Rasmus had seen her own personal fulfillment of Isaiah's prophetic invitation: "Come ye, and let us go up to the mountain of the Lord, to the house of the God of Jacob; and he will teach us of his ways, and we will walk in his paths: for out of Zion shall go forth the law, and the word of the Lord from Jerusalem" (Isaiah 2:3).

Every six months we have a marvelous general conference at which we are blessed to hear messages from our leaders, including and especially God's oracle on earth, our living prophet, seer, and revelator. May I suggest three things these twice-yearly gatherings declare to all the world.

First, they declare eagerly and unequivocally that there is again a living prophet on the earth speaking in the name of the Lord. And how we need such guidance! Our times are turbulent and difficult. We see wars internationally and distress domestically. Neighbors all around us face personal heartaches and family sorrows. Legions know fear and troubles of a hundred kinds. This reminds us that when those mists of darkness enveloped the travelers in Lehi's vision of the tree of life, it enveloped *all* of the participants—the righteous as well as the unrighteous, the young along with the elderly, the new convert and seasoned member alike. In that allegory all face opposition and travail, and only the rod of iron—the declared word of God—can bring them safely through. We *all* need that rod. We all need that word. No one is safe without it, for in its absence any can "[fall] away into forbidden paths and [be] lost," as the record says (1 Nephi 8:28; see also vv. 23–24). How grateful we are to have heard God's voice and felt the strength of that iron rod in our general conferences.

There is again a living prophet on the earth speaking in the name of the Lord. And how we need such guidance!

Not often but over the years some sources have suggested that the Brethren are out of touch in their declarations, that they don't know the issues, that some of their policies and practices are out-of-date, not relevant to our times.

As the least of those who have been sustained by you to witness the guidance of this Church firsthand, I say with all the fervor of my soul that never in my personal or professional life have I ever associated with any group who are so *in* touch, who know so profoundly the issues facing us, who look so deeply into the old, stay so open to the new, and weigh so carefully, thoughtfully, and prayerfully everything in between. I testify that the grasp this body of men and women have of moral and societal issues exceeds that of any think tank or brain trust of comparable endeavor of which I know anywhere on the earth. I bear personal witness of how thoroughly good they are, of how hard they work, and how humbly they live. It is no trivial matter for this Church to declare to the world prophecy, seership, and revelation, but we do declare it. It is true light shining in a dark world, and it shines from these proceedings.

Second, each of these conferences marks a call to action not only in our own lives but also on behalf of others around us, those who are of our own family and faith and those who are not. For example, as general conference was convening in October of 1856 here in the Salt Lake Valley, handcart companies staggering through the last freezing miles of Nebraska were soon to be stranded in the impassable snows of the high country of Wyoming. President Brigham Young's inspiring general conference message to the Saints was simply to "go and bring in those people now on the Plains."[1]

As surely as the rescue of those in need was the general conference theme of October 1856, so too is it the theme of every general conference of this Church. It may not be blizzards and frozen-earth burials that we face, but the needy are still out there—the poor and the weary, the discouraged and downhearted, those "[falling] away into [the] forbidden paths" we mentioned earlier, and multitudes who are "kept from the truth because they know not where to find it" (D&C 123:12). They are all out there with feeble knees, hands that hang down (see D&C 81:5), and bad weather setting in. They can be rescued only by those who have more and know more and can help more. And don't worry about asking, "Where are they?" They are everywhere, on our right hand and on our left, in our neighborhoods and in the workplace, in every community and county and nation of this world. Take your team and wagon; load it with your love, your testimony, and a spiritual sack of flour; then drive in any direction. The Lord will lead you to those in need if you will but embrace the gospel of Jesus Christ as it is taught in general conference. Open your heart and your hand to those trapped in the twenty-first century's equivalent of Martin's Cove and Devil's Gate. In doing so we honor the Master's repeated plea on behalf of lost sheep and lost coins and lost souls (see Luke 15).

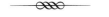

Take your team and wagon; load it with your love, your testimony, and a spiritual sack of flour; then drive in any direction. The Lord will lead you to those in need.

Finally, a general conference of the Church is a declaration to all the world that Jesus is the Christ, that He and His Father, the God and Father of us all, appeared to the boy prophet Joseph Smith in fulfillment of that ancient promise that the resurrected Jesus of Nazareth would again restore His Church on earth and again "come in like manner as [those Judean Saints had] seen him [ascend] into heaven" (Acts 1:11). Every general conference is a declaration that He condescended to come to earth in poverty and humility, to face sorrow and rejection, disappointment and death in order that we might be saved from

174

those very fates as our eternity unfolds, that "with his stripes we are healed" (Isaiah 53:5). Here prophets proclaim to every nation, kindred, tongue, and people the loving Messianic promise that "his mercy endureth for ever" (Psalm 136:1).

To you who think you are lost or without hope, or who think you have done too much that was too wrong for too long, to every one of you who worry that you are stranded somewhere on the wintry plains of life and have wrecked your handcart in the process, we call out Jehovah's unrelenting refrain, "[My] hand is stretched out still" (Isaiah 5:25; 9:17, 21). "I shall lengthen out mine arm unto them," He said, "[and even if they] deny me; nevertheless, I will be merciful unto them, . . . if they will repent and come unto me; for mine arm is lengthened out all the day long, saith the Lord God of Hosts" (2 Nephi 28:32). His mercy endureth forever, and His hand is stretched out still. His is the pure love of Christ, the charity that never faileth, that compassion which endures even when all other strength disappears (see Moroni 7:46–47).

I testify of this reaching, rescuing, merciful Jesus, that this is His redeeming Church based on His redeeming love, and that, as those in the Book of Mormon declared, "there came prophets among the people, who were sent from the Lord [to speak it]. . . . [Yea] there came prophets in the land again" (Ether 7:23; 9:28).

NOTES

From a talk given at general conference, October 2006.

1. *Deseret News,* 15 October 1856, 252; see also LeRoy R. Hafen and Ann W. Hafen, *Handcarts to Zion* (Glendale, CA: A. H. Clark Co., 1960), 120–21.

CHAPTER 19

Our Most Distinguishing Feature

More than seventy years ago President David O. McKay, then serving as a counselor in the First Presidency of the Church, asked this question to a congregation gathered for general conference: "If at this moment each one [of you] were asked to state in one sentence . . . the most distinguishing feature of the Church of Jesus Christ of Latter-day Saints, what would be your answer?

"My answer," he replied, "would be . . . divine authority by direct revelation."[1]

That divine authority is, of course, the holy priesthood.

President Gordon B. Hinckley added his testimony when he said: "[The priesthood] is a delegation of divine authority, different from all other powers and authorities on the face of the earth. . . . It is the only power on the earth that reaches beyond the veil of death. . . . Without it there could be a church in name only, [a church] lacking authority to administer in the things of God."[2]

And President James E. Faust said to BYU students in a devotional address: "[The priesthood] activates and governs all activities of the Church. Without priesthood keys and authority, there would be no church."[3]

These three brief citations—to which scores of others could be added—stress emphatically just one point: that the priesthood of God, with its keys, its ordinances, its divine origin and ability to bind in heaven what is bound on earth, is as *indispensable* to the true Church of God as it is *unique* to it. Without it there would be no Church of Jesus Christ of Latter-day Saints.

The essential function of the priesthood in linking time and eternity was made explicit by the Savior when He formed His Church during His mortal ministry. To His senior Apostle Peter He said, "I will give unto thee the keys of the kingdom of heaven: and whatsoever thou shalt bind on earth shall be bound in

The priesthood of God, with its keys, its ordinances, its divine origin and ability to bind in heaven what is bound on earth, is as indispensable *to the true Church of God as it is* unique *to it.*

heaven: and whatsoever thou shalt loose on earth shall be loosed in heaven" (Matthew 16:19). Six days later He took Peter, James, and John to a mountaintop where He was transfigured in glory before them. Then prophets from earlier dispensations, including at least Moses and Elijah (see Matthew 17:1–3), appeared in glory also and conferred the various keys and powers that each held.

Unfortunately those Apostles were soon killed or otherwise taken from the earth, and their priesthood keys were taken with them, resulting in more than 1,400 years of priesthood privation and absence of divine authority among the children of men. But part of the modern miracle and marvelous history of the latter-day Church is the return of those same earlier heavenly messengers in *our* day and the restoration of those same powers they held for the blessing of all mankind.

In May of 1829 while translating the Book of Mormon, Joseph Smith came across a reference to baptism. He discussed the matter with his scribe, Oliver Cowdery, and the two earnestly supplicated the Lord regarding the matter. Oliver wrote: "Our souls were drawn out in mighty prayer, to know how we might obtain the blessings of baptism and of the Holy Spirit. . . . *We diligently sought for . . . the authority of the holy priesthood, and the power to administer in the same.*"[4]

In response to that "mighty prayer," John the Baptist came, restoring the keys and powers of the Aaronic Priesthood. A few weeks later Peter, James, and John returned to restore the keys and powers of the Melchizedek Priesthood, including the keys of the apostleship. Then when a temple had been built to which other heavenly messengers might come, there unfolded on April 3, 1836, a modern-day equivalent of that earlier Mount of Transfiguration, part of something Elder Neal A. Maxwell once called the "Kirtland cascade" of revelation in which the Savior Himself, plus Moses, Elijah, and Elias, appeared in glory to the Prophet Joseph Smith and Oliver Cowdery and conferred keys and powers from their respective dispensations upon these men. That visit was then concluded with this thunderous declaration, "Therefore, the keys of this dispensation are committed into your hands" (D&C 110:16; see also vv. 1–15).

Little wonder that the Prophet Joseph would include in those succinct and eloquent articles of our faith, "We believe that a man must be called of God, by prophecy, and by the laying on of hands by those who are in authority, to preach the Gospel and administer in the ordinances thereof" (Articles of Faith 1:5). Clearly, acting with divine authority requires more than mere social contract. It cannot be generated by theological training or a commission from the congregation. No, in the authorized work of God there has to be power greater than that already possessed by the people in the pews or in the streets or in the seminaries—a fact that many honest religious seekers had known and openly acknowledged for generations leading up to the Restoration.

In the authorized work of God there has to be power greater than that already possessed by the people in the pews or in the streets or in the seminaries.

It is true that some few in that day did not want their ministers to claim special sacramental authority, but most people longed for priesthood sanctioned by God and were frustrated as to where they might go to find such.[5] In that spirit the revelatory return of priesthood authority through Joseph Smith should have eased centuries of anguish in those who felt what the famed Charles Wesley had the courage to say. Breaking ecclesiastically with his more famous brother John over the latter's decision to ordain without authority to do so, Charles wrote with a smile:

How easily are bishops made
By man or woman's whim:
Wesley his hands on Coke hath laid,
But who laid hands on him?[6]

In responding to that challenging question, we in the restored Church of Jesus Christ can trace the priesthood line of authority exercised by the newest deacon in the ward, the bishop who presides over him, and the prophet who presides over all of us. That line goes back in an unbroken chain to angelic ministers who came from the Son of God Himself, bearing this incomparable gift from heaven.

And, oh, how we need its blessings—as a Church and as individuals and families within the Church. Just one illustration:

I mentioned earlier the Kirtland period of Church history. The years of 1836 and 1837 were as difficult as that young Church had ever faced—financially, politically, and internally. In the midst of that stress, Joseph Smith had the remarkable prophetic prompting to send some of his ablest men (ultimately the entire Quorum of the Twelve Apostles) abroad on missions. It was a bold, inspired move, one that would in the end save the Church from the perils of the day, but in the near term it imposed great burdens on the Saints—painful for those who went away and perhaps even more painful for those who stayed at home.

I quote from Elder Robert B. Thompson:

"The day appointed for the departure of the Elders to England having arrived, I [stopped at] the house of Brother [Heber C.] Kimball to ascertain when he would start [on his journey], as I expected to accompany him two or three hundred miles, intending to spend my labors in Canada that season.

"The door being partly open, I entered and felt struck with the sight which presented itself to my view. I would have retired, thinking that I was intruding, but I felt riveted to the spot. The father was pouring out his soul to . . . [God, pleading] that He who 'careth for sparrows, and feedeth the young ravens when they cry' would supply the wants of his wife and little ones in his absence. He then, like the patriarchs, and by virtue of his office, laid his hands upon their heads individually, leaving a father's blessing upon them, . . . commending them to the care and protection of God, while he should be engaged preaching the Gospel in a foreign land. While thus engaged [in giving those blessings] his voice was almost lost in the sobs of those around [him], who [were trying in their youthful way to be strong but having a very hard time doing so.] . . . He proceeded, but his heart was too much affected to do so regularly. . . . He was obliged to stop at intervals, while . . . big tears rolled down his cheeks, an index to the feelings which reigned in his bosom. My heart was not stout enough to refrain," said Brother Thompson. "In spite of myself I wept, and mingled my tears with theirs. At the same time I felt thankful that I had the privilege of contemplating such a scene."[7]

That scene has been reenacted one way or another a thousand times, a hundred thousand times, in The Church of Jesus Christ of Latter-day Saints—a fear, a need, a call, a danger, a sickness, an accident, a death. I have been a participant in such moments. I have beheld the power of God manifest in my home and in my ministry. I have seen evil rebuked and the elements controlled. I know what it means to have mountains of difficulty move and ominous Red Seas part. I know what it means to have the destroying angel "pass by them" (D&C 89:21). To have received the authority and to have exercised the power of "the Holy Priesthood, after the Order of the Son of God" (D&C 107:3) is as great a blessing for me and for my family as I could ever hope for in this world. And that, in the end, is the meaning of the priesthood in everyday terms—its unequaled, unending, constant capacity to bless.

That, in the end, is the meaning of the priesthood in everyday terms—its unequaled, unending, constant capacity to bless.

With gratitude for such blessings I join a choir of the living and the dead in singing, "Praise to the man who communed with Jehovah!"[8] And communed with Adam; Gabriel; Moses and Moroni; Elijah; Elias; Peter, James, and John; John the Baptist; and a host of others. Truly "Jesus anointed that Prophet and Seer." May we cherish the priesthood that through him was restored, priesthood keys and ordinances by which alone the power of godliness is manifest and without which it cannot be manifest (see D&C 84:19–21). I testify of the restoration of the priesthood and the indispensable "distinguishing feature" of the true Church of God that it has always been.

NOTES

From a talk given at general conference priesthood session, April 2005.

1. In Conference Report, April 1937, 121.
2. "Priesthood Restoration," *Ensign*, October 1988, 71.
3. "Where Is the Church?" devotional address, Brigham Young University, 1 March 2005, 8.
4. Quoted in Richard Lloyd Anderson, "The Second Witness of Priesthood Restoration," *Improvement Era*, September 1968, 20; emphasis added.

5. See David F. Holland, "Priest, Pastor, Power," *Insight*, Fall 1997, 15–22, for a thorough examination of priesthood issues current in America at the time of the Restoration.

6. Quoted in C. Beaufort Moss, *The Divisions of Christendom: A Retrospect* (n.d.), 22.

7. Quoted in Orson F. Whitney, *Life of Heber C. Kimball* (Salt Lake City: Stevens & Wallis, 1945), 108–9.

8. "Praise to the Man," *Hymns of The Church of Jesus Christ of Latter-day Saints* (Salt Lake City: The Church of Jesus Christ of Latter-day Saints, 1985), no. 27. Joseph Smith had communion with many prophets and messengers from beyond the veil. For just a few of those mentioned in scripture, see D&C 128:20–21.

CHAPTER 20

"MY WORDS . . . NEVER CEASE"

The Church of Jesus Christ of Latter-day Saints is frequently accused, erroneously, of not being Christian. One major doctrine that characterizes our faith, but causes concern to some, is our bold assertion that God continues to speak His word and reveal His truth, revelations that mandate an open canon of scripture.

Some Christians, in large measure because of their genuine love for the Bible, have declared that there can be no more authorized scripture beyond the Bible. In thus pronouncing the canon of revelation closed, our friends in some other faiths shut the door on divine expression that we in The Church of Jesus Christ of Latter-day Saints hold dear: the Book of Mormon, the Doctrine and Covenants, the Pearl of Great Price, and the ongoing guidance received by God's anointed prophets and apostles. Imputing no ill will to those who take such a position, nevertheless we respectfully but resolutely reject such an unscriptural characterization of true Christianity.

One of the arguments often used in any defense of a closed canon is the New Testament passage recorded in Revelation 22:18: "For I testify unto every man that heareth the words of . . . this book, If any man shall add unto these things, God shall add unto him the plagues that are written in this book." However, there is now overwhelming consensus among virtu-ally all biblical scholars that this verse applies only to the book of Revelation, *not* the whole Bible. Those scholars of our day acknowledge a number of New Testament "books" that were almost certainly written *after* John's revelation on the Isle of Patmos was received. Included in this category are at least the books of Jude, the three Epistles of John, and probably the entire Gospel of John itself.[1] Perhaps there are even more than these.

But there is a simpler answer as to why that passage in the final book of the current New Testament cannot apply to the whole Bible. That is because the whole Bible as we know it— one collection of texts bound in a single volume—did not exist when that verse was written. For centuries after John produced his writing, the individual books of the New Testament were in circulation singly or perhaps in combinations with a few other texts but almost *never* as a complete collection. Of the entire corpus of 5,366 known Greek New Testament manuscripts, only 35 contain the whole New Testament as we now know it, and 34 of those were compiled after A.D. 1000.[2]

The fact of the matter is that virtually every prophet of the Old *and* New Testament has added scripture to that received by his predecessors. If the Old Testament words of Moses were suf-ficient, as some could have mistakenly thought them to be (see, e.g., Deuteronomy 4:2), then why, for example, the subsequent prophecies of Isaiah or of Jeremiah, who follow him? To say nothing of Ezekiel and Daniel, of Joel, Amos, and all the rest. If one revelation to one prophet in one moment of time is sufficient for *all* time, what justifies these many others? What justifies them was made clear by Jehovah Himself when He said to Moses, "My works are without end, and . . . my words . . . never cease" (Moses 1:4).

One Protestant scholar has inquired tellingly into the erroneous doctrine of a closed canon. He writes: "On what biblical or historical grounds has the inspiration of God been limited to the written documents that the church now calls its Bible? . . . If the Spirit inspired only the written documents of the first century, does that mean that the same Spirit does not speak today in the church about matters that are of significant concern?"[3] We humbly ask those same questions.

Continuing revelation does not demean or discredit existing revelation. The Old Testament does not lose its value in our eyes when we are introduced to the New Testament, and the New Testament is only enhanced when we read the Book of Mormon: Another Testament of Jesus Christ. In considering the additional scripture accepted by Latter-day Saints, we might ask: Were those early Christians who for decades had access only to the primitive Gospel of Mark (generally considered the first of the New Testament Gospels to be written)—were they offended to receive the more detailed accounts set forth later by Matthew and Luke, to say nothing of the

Continuing revelation does not demean or discredit existing revelation.

unprecedented passages and revelatory emphasis offered later yet by John? Surely they must have rejoiced that ever more convincing evidence of the divinity of Christ kept coming. And so do we rejoice.

Please do not misunderstand. We love and revere the Bible. The Bible is the word of God. It is always identified first in our canon, our "standard works." Indeed, it was a divinely ordained encounter with the fifth verse of the first chapter of the book of James that led Joseph Smith to his vision of the Father and the Son, which gave birth to the Restoration of the gospel of Jesus Christ in our time. But even then, Joseph knew the Bible alone could not be the answer to all the religious questions he and others like him had. As he said in his own words, the ministers of his community were contending—sometimes angrily—over their doctrines. "Priest [was] contending against priest, and convert [was contending] against convert . . . in a strife of words and a contest about opinions," he said. About the only thing these contending religions had in common was, ironically, a belief in the Bible, but, as Joseph wrote, "the teachers of religion of the different sects understood the same passages of scripture so differently as to destroy all confidence in settling the question [regarding which church was true] by an appeal to the Bible" (Joseph Smith—History 1:6, 12). Clearly the Bible, so frequently described at that time as "common ground," was nothing of the kind—unfortunately it was a battleground.

Thus one of the great purposes of continuing revelation through living prophets is to declare to the world through additional witnesses that the Bible is true. "*This* is written," an ancient prophet said, speaking of the Book of Mormon, "for the intent that ye may believe *that*," speaking of the Bible (Mormon 7:9; emphasis added). In one of the earliest revelations received by Joseph Smith, the Lord mentioned that same theme: "And now, behold, according to their faith in their prayers will I bring this part of my gospel to the knowledge of my people. Behold, I do not bring it to destroy that which they have received, but to build it up" (D&C 10:52; see also 20:11).

Scriptures are not the ultimate source of knowledge for Latter-day Saints. They are manifestations of the ultimate source . . . the living God.

One other point needs to be made. Since it is clear that there were Christians long before there was a New Testament or even an accumulation of the sayings of Jesus, it cannot therefore be maintained that believing in the Bible is what makes one a Christian. In the words of esteemed New Testament scholar N. T. Wright, "The risen Jesus, at the end of Matthew's Gospel, does not say, 'All authority in heaven and on earth is given to the books you are all going to write,' but [rather] 'All authority in heaven and on earth is given to me.'"[4] In other words, "Scripture itself points . . . away from itself and to the fact that final and true authority belongs to God himself."[5] So the scriptures are *not* the ultimate source of knowledge for Latter-day Saints. They are manifestations of the ultimate source. The ultimate source of knowledge and authority for a Latter-day Saint is the living God. The communication of those gifts comes from God as living, vibrant, divine revelation.[6]

This doctrine lies at the very heart of The Church of Jesus Christ of Latter-day Saints and of our message to the world. It dramatizes the significance of our sustaining the head of our

Church as a prophet, a seer, and a revelator. We believe in a God who is engaged in our lives, who is not silent, not absent, nor, as Elijah said of the god of the priests of Baal, is He "[on] a journey, or peradventure he sleepeth, and must be [awakened]" (1 Kings 18:27). In this Church, even our young Primary children recite, "We believe all that God has revealed, all that He does now reveal, and we believe that He will yet reveal many great and important things pertaining to the Kingdom of God" (Articles of Faith 1:9).

In declaring new scripture and continuing revelation, we pray we will never be arrogant or insensitive. But after a sacred vision in a now sacred grove answered in the affirmative the question "Does God exist?" what Joseph Smith and The Church of Jesus Christ of Latter-day Saints force us to face is the next interrogative, which necessarily follows: "Does He speak?" We bring the good news that He does and that He has. With a love and affection born of our Christianity, we invite all to inquire into the wonder of what God has said since biblical times and is saying even now.

I testify that the heavens are open. I testify that Joseph Smith was and is a prophet of God, that the Book of Mormon is truly another testament of Jesus Christ. I testify that Thomas S. Monson is God's prophet, a modern apostle with the keys of the kingdom in his hands, a man upon whom I personally have seen the mantle fall. I testify that the presence of such authorized, prophetic voices and ongoing canonized revelations have been at the heart of the Christian message whenever the authorized ministry of Christ has been on the earth. I testify that such a ministry *is* on the earth again, and it is found in this, The Church of Jesus Christ of Latter-day Saints.

In our heartfelt devotion to Jesus of Nazareth as the very

Son of God, the Savior of the world, we invite all to examine what we have received of Him, to join with us, drinking deeply at the "well of water springing up into everlasting life" (John 4:14), these constantly flowing reminders that God lives, that He loves us, and that He speaks. I express the deepest personal thanks that His works never end and His "words . . . never cease."

NOTES

From a talk given at general conference, April 2008.

1. See Stephen E. Robinson, *Are Mormons Christians?* (Salt Lake City: Bookcraft, 1991), 46. The issue of canon is discussed on pages 45–56. *Canon* is defined as "an authoritative list of books accepted as Holy Scripture" (*Merriam Webster's Collegiate Dictionary*, 11th ed. [2003], "canon").

2. See Bruce M. Metzger, *Manuscripts of the Greek Bible: An Introduction to Greek Paleography* (New York: Oxford University Press, 1981), 54–55; see also *Are Mormons Christians?* 46.

3. Lee M. McDonald, *The Formation of the Christian Biblical Canon*, rev. ed. (Peabody, MA: Hendrickson Publishers, 1995), 255–56.

4. N. T. Wright, *The Last Word: Beyond the Bible Wars to a New Understanding of the Authority of Scripture* (San Francisco, CA: Harper SanFrancisco, 2005), xi.

5. Wright, *Last Word*, 24.

6. For a full essay on this subject, see Dallin H. Oaks, "Scripture Reading and Revelation," *Ensign*, January 1995, 6–9.

THE SOURCE OF ALL HEALING

CHAPTER 21

"ABIDE IN ME"

I would like to thank every missionary who has ever labored in this transcendent latter-day undertaking we have been given. The rolling forth of the restored gospel is a miracle in every sense of the word, and not the least of the miracle is that a significant portion of it rolls forward on the shoulders of nineteen-year-olds! Clean, clear, bright-eyed missionaries, laboring two-by-two, have become a living symbol of this Church everywhere. They themselves are the first gospel message their investigators encounter—and what a message that is. Everyone knows who they are, and those who know them the best, love them the most.

I wish you could meet the sister called to serve from her native Argentina. Wanting to do everything possible to finance her own mission, she sold her violin, her most prized and nearly sole earthly possession. She said simply, "God will bless me with another violin after I have blessed His children with the gospel of Jesus Christ."

I wish you could meet the Chilean elder who, living without family in a boarding school, happened upon a Book of Mormon and started reading it that very evening. Reminiscent of Parley P. Pratt's experience, he read insatiably—nonstop through the night. With the breaking of day, he was overwhelmed with a profound sense of peace and a new spirit of hope. He determined to find out where this book had come from and who had written its marvelous pages. Thirteen months later he was on a mission.

I wish you could meet the marvelous young man who came to one of our missions in Chile from Bolivia, arriving with no matching clothing and shoes three sizes too large for him. He was a little older than many of the elders because he was the sole breadwinner in his home and it had taken some time to earn money for his mission. He raised chickens and sold the eggs door-to-door. Then, just as his call finally came, his widowed mother faced an emergency appendectomy. Our young friend gave every cent of the money he had earned for his mission to pay for his mother's surgery and postoperative care, then quietly rounded up what used clothing he could from friends and arrived at the Missionary Training Center in Santiago on schedule. I can assure you that his clothes now match, his shoes now fit, and both he and his mother are safe and sound, temporally as well as spiritually.

And so they come, from your homes all over the world. Included in such a long list of dedicated servants of the Lord is an increasing number of senior couples who make an indispensable contribution to the work. How we love and need couples in virtually every mission of this Church! Those of you who can, put away your golf clubs, don't worry about the stock market, realize that your grandchildren will still be your grandchildren when you return—and go! We promise you the experience of a lifetime.

Let me say something of the marvelous members of the Church themselves. In the reorganization of a rather far-flung stake recently, I felt the Lord's prompting to call a man to the stake presidency who, I had been told, owned a bicycle but no automobile. Many leaders across the Church don't have cars, but I was nevertheless worried about what that might mean for this man in this particular stake. In my terminally ill Spanish I pursued the interview, then said, *"Hermano, no tiene un auto?"* With a smile and not a second's hesitation he replied, *"No tengo un auto; pero yo tengo pies, yo tengo fe."* ("I do not have a car, but I do have feet and I do have faith.") He then said he could ride the bus, ride his bicycle, or walk, *"como los misioneros,"* he smiled—"like the missionaries." And so he does.

I once held a mission district conference on the island of Chiloe, an interior location in the south of Chile that gets few visitors. Imagine the responsibility I felt in addressing these beautiful people when it was pointed out to me that a very elderly man seated near the front of the chapel had set out on foot at five o'clock that morning, walking for four hours to be in his seat by nine o'clock, for a meeting that was not scheduled to begin until eleven o'clock. He said he wanted to get a good seat. I looked into his eyes, thought of times in my life when I had been either too casual or too late, and thought of Jesus' phrase, "I have not found so great faith, no, not in Israel" (Matthew 8:10).

The Punta Arenas Chile Stake is the Church's southernmost stake anywhere on this planet, its outermost borders stretching toward Antarctica. Any stake farther south would have to be staffed by penguins. For the Punta Arenas Saints it is a 4,200-mile round-trip bus ride to the Santiago Temple. For a husband and wife it can take up to 20 percent of an annual local income just for the transportation alone. Only 50 people can be accommodated on the bus, but for every excursion 250 others come out to hold a brief service with them the morning of their departure.

Pause for a minute and ask yourself when was the last time you stood on a cold, windswept parking lot adjacent to the Strait of Magellan just to sing with, pray for, and cheer on their way those who were going to the temple, hoping your savings would allow you to go next time? One hundred ten hours, seventy of those on dusty, bumpy, unfinished roads looping out through Argentina's wild Patagonia. What does 110 hours on a bus feel like? I honestly don't know, but I do know that some of us get nervous if we live more than 110 miles from a temple or if the services there take more than 110 minutes. While we are teaching the principle of tithing to, praying with, and building ever more temples for just such distant Latter-day Saints, perhaps the rest of us can do more to enjoy the blessings and wonder of the temple regularly when so many temples are increasingly within our reach.

When was the last time you stood on a cold, windswept parking lot adjacent to the Strait of Magellan just to sing with, pray for, and cheer on their way those who were going to the temple, hoping your savings would allow you to go next time?

And that leads me to my final point. For the Church at large, we have so many things come to mind when we look back on the visionary ministry of President Gordon B. Hinckley, including (perhaps especially) the vast expansion of temples and temple building. But I dare say, it is likely that we will remember him at least as emphatically for his determination to retain in permanent activity the converts who join this Church. No modern prophet addressed this issue more directly nor expected more from us in seeing that it happen. I remember a time when, with a twinkle in his eye and a hand smacking the table in front of him, he said to the Twelve, "Brethren, when my life is finished and the final services are concluding, I am going to rise up as I go by, look each of you in the eye, and say, 'How are we doing on retention?'"

This subject brings us full circle, linking the kind of true, deep conversion the missionaries are striving to bring with the greater commitment and devotion being seen in wonderful members all over the Church.

Christ said, "I am the true vine, and . . . ye are the branches" (John 15:1, 5). "Abide in me, and I in you. As the branch cannot bear fruit of itself, except it abide in the vine; no more can ye, except ye abide in me" (John 15:4).

"Abide in me" is an understandable and beautiful enough concept in the elegant English of the King James Bible, but "abide" is not a word we use much anymore. So I gained even more appreciation for this admonition from the Lord when I was introduced to the translation of this passage in another language. In Spanish that familiar phrase is rendered *"permaneced en mi."* Like the English verb "abide," *permanecer* means "to remain, to stay," but even gringos like me can recognize the root cognate there of "permanence." The sense of this then is "stay—but stay *forever*." That is the call of the gospel message to everyone in the world. Come, but come to remain. Come with conviction and endurance. Come permanently, for your sake and the sake of all the generations who must follow you, and we will help each other be strong to the very end.

"He who picks up one end of the stick, picks up the other," my marvelous mission president taught in his very first message to us.[1] And that is the way it is supposed to be when we join this, the true and living Church of the true and living God. When we join The Church of Jesus Christ of Latter-day Saints, we board the Good Ship *Zion* and sail with her wherever she goes until she comes into that millennial port. *We stay in the boat,* through squalls and stills, through storms and sunburn, because that is the only way to the promised land. This Church is the Lord's vehicle for crucial doctrines, ordinances, covenants, and keys that are essential to exaltation, and one cannot be fully faithful to the gospel of Jesus Christ without striving to be faithful in the Church, which is its earthly institutional manifestation. To new convert and longtime member alike, we declare in the spirit of Nephi's powerful valedictory exhortation: "Ye have entered in by the gate; . . . [but] now, . . . after ye have gotten into this strait and narrow path, I would ask if all is done? Behold, I say unto you, Nay; . . . press forward with a steadfastness in Christ, . . . and endure to the end, behold, thus . . . ye shall have eternal life" (2 Nephi 31:18–20).

One cannot be fully faithful to the gospel of Jesus Christ without striving to be faithful in the Church, which is its earthly institutional manifestation.

Jesus said, "Without me ye can do nothing" (John 15:5). I testify that is God's truth. Christ is everything to us and we are to "abide" in Him permanently, unyieldingly, steadfastly, forever. For the fruit of the gospel to blossom and bless our lives, we must be firmly attached to Him, the Savior of us all, and to this His Church, which bears His holy name. He is the vine that is our true source of strength and the only source of eternal life. In Him we not only will endure but also will prevail and triumph in this holy cause that will never fail us.

NOTES

From a talk given at general conference, April 3, 2004.

1.   Marion D. Hanks quoting Harry Emerson Fosdick, *Living Under Tension* (New York: Harper & Brothers, 1941), 111.

CHAPTER 22

THE ATONEMENT OF
JESUS CHRIST

As a young missionary, Elder Orson F. Whitney, who later served in the Quorum of the Twelve Apostles, had a dream so powerful that it changed his life forever. He later wrote: "One night I dreamed . . . that I was in the Garden of Gethsemane, a witness of the Savior's agony. . . . I stood behind a tree in the foreground. . . . Jesus, with Peter, James, and John, came through a little wicket gate at my right. Leaving the three Apostles there, after telling them to kneel and pray, He passed over to the other side, where He also knelt and prayed . . . : 'Oh my Father, if it be possible, let this cup pass from me; nevertheless not as I will but as Thou wilt.'

"As He prayed the tears streamed down His face, which was [turned] toward me. I was so moved at the sight that I wept also, out of pure sympathy with His great sorrow. My whole heart went out to Him. I loved Him with all my soul and longed to be with Him as I longed for nothing else.

"Presently He arose and walked to where those Apostles were kneeling—fast asleep! He shook them gently, awoke them, and in a tone of tender reproach, untinctured by the least show of anger or scolding, asked them if they could not watch with Him one hour. . . .

"Returning to His place, He prayed again and then went back and found them again sleeping. Again He awoke them, admonished them, and returned and prayed as before. Three times this happened, until I was perfectly familiar with His appearance—face, form, and movements. He was of noble stature and of majestic mien . . . the very God that He was and is, yet as meek and lowly as a little child.

"All at once the circumstance seemed to change. . . . Instead of before, it was after the Crucifixion, and the Savior, with those three Apostles, now stood together in a group at my left. They were about to depart and ascend into heaven. I could endure it no longer. I ran from behind the tree, fell at His feet, clasped Him around the knees, and begged Him to take me with Him.

"I shall never forget the kind and gentle manner in which He stooped and raised me up and embraced me. It was so vivid, so real that I felt the very warmth of His bosom against which I rested. Then He said: 'No, my son; these have finished their work, and they may go with me; but you must stay and finish yours.' Still I clung to Him. Gazing up into His face—for He was taller than I—I besought Him most earnestly: 'Well, promise me that I will come to You at the last.' He smiled sweetly and tenderly and replied: 'That will depend entirely upon yourself.' I awoke with a sob in my throat, and it was morning."[1]

This tender, personal glimpse of the Savior's loving sacrifice is a fitting introduction to the significance of the Atonement of Jesus Christ. Indeed the Atonement of the Only Begotten Son of God in the flesh is the crucial foundation upon which all Christian doctrine rests and the greatest expression of divine love this world has ever been given. Its importance in The Church of Jesus Christ of Latter-day Saints cannot be overstated. Every other principle, commandment, and virtue of the restored gospel draws its significance from this pivotal event.[2]

The Atonement of the Only Begotten Son of God in the flesh is the crucial foundation upon which all Christian doctrine rests.

The Atonement was the foreordained but voluntary act of the Only Begotten Son of God in which He offered His life and spiritual anguish as a redeeming ransom for the effect of the Fall of Adam upon all mankind and for the personal sins of all who repent.

The literal meaning of the English word *atonement* is self-evident: at-one-ment, the bringing together of things that have been separated or estranged. The Atonement of Jesus Christ was indispensable because of the separating transgression, or Fall, of Adam, which brought two kinds of death into the world when Adam and Eve partook of the fruit of the tree of knowledge of good and evil (see Genesis 2:9; 3). Physical death brought the separation of the spirit from the body, and spiritual death brought the estrangement of both the spirit and the body from God. As a result of the Fall, all persons born into mortality would suffer these two kinds of death. But we must remember the Fall was an essential part of Heavenly Father's divine plan. Without it no mortal children would have been born to Adam and Eve, and there would have been no human family to experience opposition and growth, moral agency, and the joy of resurrection, redemption, and eternal life (see 2 Nephi 2:22–27; Moses 5:11).

The need for this Fall and for an atonement to compensate for it was explained in a premortal Council in Heaven at which the spirits of the entire human family attended and over which God the Father presided. It was in this premortal setting that Christ volunteered to honor the moral agency of all humankind even as He atoned for their sins. In the process, He would return to the Father all glory for such redemptive love (see Moses 4:1–2; Abraham 3:22–27).

This infinite Atonement of Christ was possible because (1) He was the only sinless man ever to live on this earth and therefore was not subject to the spiritual death resulting from sin, (2) He was the Only Begotten of the Father and therefore possessed the attributes of godhood that gave Him power over physical death (see John 5:26–29; 2 Nephi 9:5–12; Alma 34:9–14), and (3) He was apparently the only one sufficiently humble and willing in the premortal council to be foreordained to that service.[3]

Some gifts coming from the Atonement are universal, infinite, and unconditional. These include His ransom for Adam's original transgression so that no member of the human family is held responsible for that sin (see Articles of Faith 1:2). Another universal gift is the resurrection from the dead of every man, woman, and child who lives, has ever lived, or ever will live on earth.

Other aspects of Christ's atoning gift are conditional. They depend on one's diligence in keeping God's commandments. For example, while all members of the human family are freely given a reprieve from Adam's sin through no effort of their own, they are not given a reprieve from their own sins unless they pledge faith in Christ, repent of those sins, are baptized in His name, receive the gift of the Holy Ghost and confirmation into Christ's Church, and press forward in faithful endurance the remainder of life's journey. Of this personal challenge, Christ said, "For behold, I, God, have suffered these things for all, that they might not suffer if they would repent; but if they would not repent they must suffer even as I" (D&C 19:16–17).

Furthermore, although the resurrection of the body is a free and universal gift from Christ, a result of His victory over death, the nature of the resurrected body (or "degree of glory" given it), as well as the time of one's resurrection, is affected directly by one's faithfulness in this life. The Apostle Paul made clear, for example, that those fully committed to Christ will "rise first" in the Resurrection (1 Thessalonians 4:16). Modern revelation clarifies the different orders of resurrected bodies (see D&C 76:50–113; compare 1 Corinthians 15:40–42), promising the highest degree of glory only to those who adhere to the principles and ordinances of the gospel of Jesus Christ (see D&C 76:50–70; 88:4, 27–29; 132:21–24).

Neither the unconditional nor the conditional blessings of the Atonement are available except through the grace of Christ.

Of course neither the unconditional nor the conditional blessings of the Atonement are available except through the grace of Christ. Obviously the unconditional blessings of the Atonement are unearned, but the conditional ones are not fully merited either. By living faithfully and keeping the commandments of God, one can receive additional privileges; but they are still given freely, not technically earned. The Book of

Mormon declares emphatically that "there is no flesh that can dwell in the presence of God, save it be through the merits, and mercy, and grace of the Holy Messiah" (2 Nephi 2:8).

By this same grace, God provides for the salvation of little children, the mentally impaired, those who lived without hearing the gospel of Jesus Christ, and so forth. These are redeemed by the universal power of the Atonement of Christ and will have the opportunity to receive the fulness of the gospel after death, in the spirit world, where spirits reside while awaiting the Resurrection (see Alma 40:11; D&C 138; compare Luke 23:43; John 5:25).

To begin to meet the demands of the Atonement, the sinless Christ went into the Garden of Gethsemane, as Elder Whitney saw in his dream, there to bear the agony of soul only He could bear. He "began to be sore amazed, and to be very heavy," saying to Peter, James, and John, "My soul is exceeding sorrowful, unto death" (Mark 14:33–34). Why? Because He suffered "the pains of all men, yea, the pains of every living creature, both men, women, and children, who belong to the family of Adam" (2 Nephi 9:21). He experienced "temptations, and pain of body, hunger, thirst, and fatigue, even more than man can suffer, except it be unto death; for behold, blood cometh from every pore, so great [was] his anguish" (Mosiah 3:7).

Through this suffering, Jesus redeemed the souls of all men, women, and children "that his bowels may be filled with mercy, according to the flesh, that he may know according to the flesh how to succor his people according to their infirmities" (Alma 7:12). In doing so, Christ "descended below all things"— including every kind of sickness, infirmity, and dark despair experienced by every mortal being—in order that He might comprehend all things, "that he might be in all and through all things, the light of truth" (D&C 88:6).

The utter loneliness and excruciating pain of the Atonement begun in Gethsemane reached its zenith when, after unspeakable abuse at the hands of Roman soldiers and others, Christ cried from the cross, "Eli, Eli, lama sabachthani? that is to say, My God, my God, why hast thou forsaken me?" (Matthew 27:46). In the depths of that anguish, even nature itself convulsed. "There was a darkness over all the earth. . . . And the sun was darkened" (Luke 23:44–45). "And, behold, the veil of the temple was rent in twain from the top to the bottom; and the earth did quake, and the rocks rent" (Matthew 27:51), causing many to exclaim, "The God of nature suffers" (1 Nephi 19:12). Finally, even the seemingly unbearable had been borne, and Jesus said, "It is finished" (John 19:30). "Father, into thy hands I commend my spirit" (Luke 23:46). Someday, somewhere, every human tongue will be called upon to confess as did a Roman centurion who witnessed all of this, "Truly this was the Son of God" (Matthew 27:54).

To the thoughtful woman and man, it is "a matter of surpassing wonder"[4] that the voluntary and merciful sacrifice of a single being could satisfy the infinite and eternal demands of justice, atone for every human transgression and misdeed, and thereby sweep all humankind into the encompassing arms of His merciful embrace. But so it is.

To quote President John Taylor: "In a manner to us incomprehensible and inexplicable, He bore the weight of the sins of the whole world; not only of Adam, but of his posterity; and in doing that, opened the kingdom of heaven, not only to all believers and all who obeyed the law of God, but to more than one-half of the human family who die before they come to years of maturity, as well as to [those] who . . . [die] without [the] law."[5]

As Elder Whitney felt regarding this majestic gift and the giver of it, may we so feel: "I was so moved at the [gift] that I wept . . . out of pure sympathy. . . . My whole heart went out to Him. I loved Him with all my soul and longed to be with Him as I longed for nothing else." Having already offered the Atonement in our behalf, Christ has done His part to make that longing a reality. The rest will depend entirely upon ourselves.

NOTES

From an article published in Ensign, March 2008.

1. "The Divinity of Jesus Christ," *Improvement Era*, January 1926, 224–25; see also *Ensign*, December 2003, 10; punctuation, capitalization, and spelling standardized.
2. See *Teachings of Presidents of the Church: Joseph Smith* (Salt Lake City: The Church of Jesus Christ of Latter-day Saints, 2007), 49.
3. See James E. Talmage, *Jesus the Christ*, 3rd ed. (Salt Lake City: Deseret Book, 1916), 21–22.
4. James E. Talmage, *Articles of Faith*, 12th ed. (Salt Lake City: Deseret Book, 1924), 77.
5. John Taylor, *The Mediation and Atonement* (Salt Lake City: Deseret News Company, 1882), 148–49; capitalization standardized.

CHAPTER 23

The Only True God and Jesus Christ Whom He Hath Sent

V arious crosscurrents of our times have brought increasing public attention to The Church of Jesus Christ of
Latter-day Saints. The Lord told the ancients this
latter-day work would be "a marvellous work and a wonder"
(Isaiah 29:14), and it is. But even as we invite one and all to
examine closely the *marvel* of it, there is one thing we would
not like anyone to *wonder* about—that is whether or not we are
"Christians."

By and large much of the controversy in this matter has
swirled around a major doctrinal issue—our view of the
Godhead. With a desire to increase understanding and unequivocally declare our Christianity, I wish to examine carefully our
understanding of this matter.

Our first and foremost article of faith in The Church of Jesus
Christ of Latter-day Saints is "We believe in God, the Eternal
Father, and in His Son, Jesus Christ, and in the Holy Ghost"

(Articles of Faith 1:1). We believe these three divine persons constituting a single Godhead are united in purpose, in manner, in testimony, in mission. We believe Them to be filled with the same godly sense of mercy and love, justice and grace, patience, forgiveness, and redemption. I think it is accurate to say we believe They are one in every significant and eternal aspect imaginable *except* believing Them to be three persons combined in one substance, a Trinitarian notion never set forth in the scriptures because it is not true.

Indeed no less a source than the stalwart *Harper's Bible Dictionary* records that "the formal doctrine of the Trinity as it was defined by the great church councils of the fourth and fifth centuries is *not* to be found in the [New Testament]."[1]

So any criticism that The Church of Jesus Christ of Latter-day Saints does not hold the contemporary Christian view of God, Jesus, and the Holy Ghost is *not* a comment about our commitment to Christ but rather a recognition (accurate, I might add) that our view of the Godhead breaks with post-New Testament Christian history and returns to the doctrine taught by Jesus Himself. Now, a word about that post-New Testament history might be helpful.

Our view of the Godhead breaks with post-New Testament Christian history and returns to the doctrine taught by Jesus Himself.

In the year A.D. 325 the Roman emperor Constantine convened the Council of Nicaea to address—among other things—the growing issue of God's alleged "trinity in unity." What emerged from the heated contentions of churchmen, philosophers, and ecclesiastical dignitaries came to be known (after another 125 years and three more major councils: Constantinople, A.D. 381; Ephesus, A.D. 431.; Chalcedon, A.D. 451) as the Nicene Creed, with later reformulations such as the Athanasian Creed. These various evolutions and iterations of creeds—and others to come over the centuries—declared the Father, Son, and Holy Ghost to be abstract, absolute, transcendent, immanent, consubstantial, coeternal, and unknowable, without body, parts, or passions and dwelling outside space and time. In such creeds all three members are separate persons, but they are a single being, the oft-noted "mystery of the trinity." They are three distinct persons, yet not three Gods but one. All three persons are incomprehensible, yet it is one God who is incomprehensible.

We agree with our critics on at least that point—that such a formulation for Divinity is truly incomprehensible. With such a confusing definition of God being imposed upon the church, little wonder that a fourth-century monk cried out, "Woe is me! They have taken my God away from me, . . . and I know not whom to adore or to address."[2] How *are* we to trust, love, worship, to say nothing of strive to be like, One who is incomprehensible and unknowable? What of Jesus' prayer to His Father in Heaven that "this is life eternal, that they might *know* thee the only true God, and Jesus Christ, whom *thou* hast sent"? (John 17:3; emphasis added).

It is not our purpose to demean any person's belief nor the doctrine of any religion. We extend to all the same respect for their doctrine that we are asking for ours. (That, too, is an article of our faith.) But if one says we are not Christians because we do not hold a fourth- or fifth-century view of the Godhead, then what of those first Christian Saints, many of whom were eyewitnesses of the living Christ, who did not hold such a view either?³ We declare it is self-evident from the scriptures that the Father, the Son, and the Holy Ghost are separate persons, three divine beings, noting such unequivocal illustrations as the Savior's great Intercessory Prayer just mentioned, His baptism at the hands of John, the experience on the Mount of Transfiguration, and the martyrdom of Stephen—to name just four.

With these New Testament sources and more (see, for example, John 12:27–30; John 14:26; Romans 8:34; Hebrews 1:1–3) ringing in our ears, it may be redundant to ask what Jesus meant when He said, "The Son can do nothing of himself, but what he seeth the Father do" (John 5:19; see also John 14:10). On another occasion He said, "I came down from heaven, not to do mine own will, but the will of him that sent me" (John 6:38). Of His antagonists He said, "[They have] . . . seen and hated both me and my Father" (John 15:24). And there is, of course, that always deferential subordination to His Father that had Jesus say, "Why callest thou me good? there is none good but one, that is, God" (Matthew 19:17). "My father is greater than I" (John 14:28).

To whom was Jesus pleading so fervently all those years, including in such anguished cries as "O my Father, if it be possible, let this cup pass from me" (Matthew 26:39) and "My God, my God, why hast thou forsaken me"? (Matthew 27:46). To acknowledge the scriptural evidence that otherwise perfectly united members of the Godhead are nevertheless separate and distinct beings is not to be guilty of polytheism; it is, rather, part of the great revelation Jesus came to deliver concerning the nature of divine beings. Perhaps the Apostle Paul said it best: "Christ Jesus . . . being in the form of God, thought it not robbery to be equal with God" (Philippians 2:5–6).

A related reason The Church of Jesus Christ of Latter-day Saints is excluded from the Christian category by some is because we believe, as did the ancient prophets and Apostles, in an embodied—but certainly glorified—God.[4] To those who criticize this scripturally based belief, I ask at least rhetorically: If the idea of an embodied God is repugnant, why are the central doctrines and singularly most distinguishing characteristics of all Christianity the Incarnation, the Atonement, and the physical Resurrection of the Lord Jesus Christ? If having a body is not only not needed but not desirable by Deity, why did the Redeemer of mankind redeem *His* body from the grasp of death and the grave, guaranteeing it would never again be separated from His spirit in time or eternity? (see Romans 6:9; Alma 11:45). *Any who dismiss the concept of an embodied God dismiss both the mortal and the resurrected Christ.* No one claiming to be a true Christian will want to do that.

If having a body is not only not needed but not desirable by Deity, why did the Redeemer of mankind redeem His body from the grasp of death and the grave?

To anyone who has wondered regarding our Christianity, I bear this witness. I testify that Jesus Christ is the literal, living Son of our literal, living God. This Jesus is our Savior and Redeemer who, under the guidance of the Father, was the Creator of heaven and earth and all things that in them are. I bear witness that He was born of a virgin mother, that in His lifetime He performed mighty miracles observed by legions of His disciples and by His enemies as well.

I testify that He had power over death because He was divine but that He willingly subjected Himself to death for our sake because for a period of time He was also mortal. I declare that in His willing submission to death He took upon Himself the sins of the world, paying an infinite price for every sorrow and sickness, every heartache and unhappiness from Adam to the end of the world. In doing so He conquered both the grave physically and hell spiritually and set the human family free. I bear witness that He was literally resurrected from the tomb and, after ascending to His Father to complete the process of that Resurrection, He appeared, repeatedly, to hundreds of disciples in the Old World and in the New.

I know He is the Holy One of Israel, the Messiah who will one day come again in final glory, to reign on earth as Lord of lords and King of kings. I know that there is no other name given under heaven whereby a man can be saved and that only by relying wholly upon His merits, mercy, and everlasting grace (see 1 Nephi 10:6; 2 Nephi 2:8; 31:19; Moroni 6:4; JST, Romans 3:24) can we gain eternal life.

My additional testimony regarding this resplendent doctrine is that in preparation for His millennial latter-day reign, Jesus has already come, more than once, in embodied majestic glory. In the spring of 1820, a fourteen-year-old boy, confused by many of these very doctrines that still confuse much of Christendom, went into a grove of trees to pray. In answer to that earnest prayer offered at such a tender age, the Father and the Son appeared as embodied, glorified beings to the boy prophet Joseph Smith. That day marked the beginning of the return of the true, New Testament gospel of the Lord Jesus Christ and the restoration of other prophetic truths offered from Adam down to the present day.

I testify that my witness of these things is true and that the heavens are open to all who seek the same confirmation. Through the Holy Spirit of Truth, may we *all* know "the only true God, and Jesus Christ, whom [He has] sent" (John 17:3).

NOTES

From a talk given at general conference, October 2007.

1. In *Harper's Bible Dictionionary*, Paul J. Achtemeier, ed. (San Francisco: Harper & Row, 1985), 1099; emphasis added.

2. Quoted in Owen Chadwick, *Western Asceticism* (Philadelphia, PA: Westminster Press, 1958), 235.

3. For a thorough discussion of this issue, see Stephen E. Robinson, *Are Mormons Christians?* (Salt Lake City: Bookcraft, 1991), 71–89; see also Robert Millet, *Getting at the Truth* (Salt Lake City: Deseret Book, 2004), 106–22.

4. See David L. Paulsen, "Early Christian Belief in a Corporeal Deity: Origen and Augustine as Reluctant Witnesses," *Harvard Theological Review*, vol. 83, no. 2 (1990): 105–16; David L. Paulsen, "The Doctrine of Divine Embodiment: Restoration, Judeo-Christian, and Philosophical Perspectives," *BYU Studies*, vol. 35, no. 4 (1996): 7–94; James L. Kugel, *The God of Old: Inside the Lost World of the Bible* (New York: Free Press, 2003), xi-xii, 5–6, 104–6, 134–35; Clark Pinnock, *Most Moved Mover: A Theology of God's Openness* (Grand Rapids, MI: Baker Academic, 2001), 33–34.

CHAPTER 24

THE GRANDEUR OF GOD

Of the many magnificent purposes served in the life and ministry of the Lord Jesus Christ, one great aspect of that mission often goes uncelebrated. His followers did not understand it fully at the time, and many in modern Christianity do not grasp it now, but the Savior Himself spoke of it repeatedly and emphatically. It is the grand truth that in all that Jesus came to say and do, including and especially in His atoning suffering and sacrifice, He was showing us who and what God our Eternal Father is like, how completely devoted He is to His children in every age and nation. In word and in deed Jesus was trying to reveal and make personal to us the true nature of His Father, our Father in Heaven.

He did this at least in part because then and now all of us need to know God more fully in order to love Him more deeply and obey Him more completely. As both Old and New Testaments declare, "The first of all the commandments is . . .

thou shalt love the Lord thy God with all thy heart, and with all thy soul, and with all thy mind, and with all thy strength: this is the first [and great] commandment" (Mark 12:29–30; see also Matthew 22:37–38; Deuteronomy 6:5).

All of us need to know God more fully in order to love Him more deeply and obey Him more completely.

Little wonder then that the Prophet Joseph Smith taught: "It is the first principle of the gospel to know for a certainty the character of God." "I want you all to know Him," he said, "and to be familiar with Him."[1] We must have "a correct idea of his . . . perfections, and attributes," an admiration for "the excellency of [His] character."[2] Thus the first phrase we utter in the declaration of our faith is, "We believe in God, the Eternal Father" (Articles of Faith 1:1). So, emphatically, did Jesus. Even as He acknowledged His own singular role in the divine plan, the Savior nevertheless insisted on this prayerful preamble: "And this is life eternal, that they might know thee the only true God" (John 17:3).

After generations of prophets had tried to teach the family of man the will and the way of the Father, usually with little success, God, in His ultimate effort to have us know Him, sent to earth His Only Begotten and perfect Son, created in His very likeness and image, to live and serve among mortals in the everyday rigors of life.

To come to earth with such a responsibility, to stand in place of Elohim—speaking as He would speak, judging and serving, loving and warning, forbearing and forgiving as He would do—this is a duty of such staggering proportions that you and I cannot comprehend such a thing. But in the loyalty and determination that would be characteristic of a divine child, Jesus could comprehend it and He did it. Then, when the praise and honor began to come, He humbly directed all adulation to the Father.

"The Father . . . doeth the works," He said in earnest. "The Son can do nothing of himself, but what he seeth the Father do: for what things soever [the Father] doeth, these also doeth the Son likewise" (John 14:10; 5:19). On another occasion He said: "I speak that which I have seen with my Father." "I do nothing of myself; but as my Father hath taught me." "I came down from heaven, not to do mine own will, but the will of him that sent me" (John 8:38, 28; 6:38).

I make my own heartfelt declaration of God our Eternal Father because some in the contemporary world suffer from a distressing misconception of Him. Among these there is a tendency to feel distant from the Father, even estranged from Him, if they believe in Him at all. And if they do believe, many moderns say they might feel comfortable in the arms of Jesus, but they are uneasy contemplating the stern encounter of God.[3] Through a misreading (and surely, in some cases, a mistranslation) of the Bible, these see God the Father and Jesus Christ His Son as operating very differently, this in spite of the fact that in both the Old Testament and the New, the Son of God is one and the same, acting as He always does under the direction of the Father, who is Himself "the same yesterday, today, and forever" (for example, 2 Nephi 27:23; Moroni 10:19; D&C 20:12).

In reflecting on these misconceptions we realize that one of the remarkable contributions of the Book of Mormon is its seamless, perfectly consistent view of divinity throughout that majestic book. Here there is no Malachi-to-Matthew gap, no pause while we shift theological gears, no misreading the God who is urgently, lovingly, faithfully at work on every page of that record from its Old Testament beginning to its New Testament end. Yes, in an effort to give the world back its Bible and a correct view of Deity with it, what we have in the Book of Mormon is a uniform view of God in all His glory and goodness, all His richness and complexity—including and especially as again demonstrated through a personal appearance of His Only Begotten Son, Jesus Christ.

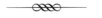

One of the remarkable contributions of the Book of Mormon is its seamless, perfectly consistent view of divinity throughout that majestic book.

How grateful we are for all the scriptures, especially the scriptures of the Restoration, that teach us the majesty of each member of the Godhead. How we would thrill, for example, if all the world would receive and embrace the view of the Father so movingly described in the Pearl of Great Price.

There, in the midst of a grand vision of humankind that heaven opened to his view, Enoch, observing both the blessings and challenges of mortality, turns his gaze toward the Father and is stunned to see Him weeping. He says in wonder and amazement to this most powerful Being in the universe: "How is it that thou canst weep[?] . . . Thou art just [and] merciful and kind forever; . . . Peace . . . is the habitation of thy throne; and mercy shall go before thy face and have no end; how is it thou canst weep?"

Looking out on the events of almost any day, God replies: "Behold these thy brethren; they are the workmanship of mine own hands. . . . I gave unto them . . . [a] commandment, that they should love one another, and that they should choose me, their Father; but behold, they are without affection, and they hate their own blood. . . . Wherefore should not the heavens weep, seeing these shall suffer?" (Moses 7:29–33, 37).

That single, riveting scene does more to teach the true nature of God than any theological treatise could ever convey. It also helps us understand much more emphatically that vivid moment in the Book of Mormon allegory of the olive tree when, after digging and dunging, watering and weeding, trimming, pruning, transplanting, and grafting, the great Lord of the vineyard throws down his spade and his pruning shears and weeps, crying out to any who will listen, "What could I have done more for my vineyard?" (Jacob 5:41; see also vv. 47, 49).

What an indelible image of God's engagement in our lives! What anguish in a parent when His children do not choose Him or "the gospel of God" He sent! (Romans 1:1). How easy to love someone who so singularly loves us!

In His own ministry, Jesus did not come to improve God's view of man nearly so much as He came to improve man's view of God and to plead with them to love their Heavenly Father as He has always and will always love them. The plan of God, the power of God, the holiness of God, yes, even the anger and the judgment of God they had occasion to understand. But the love of God, the profound depth of His devotion to His children, they still did not fully know—until Christ came.

So feeding the hungry, healing the sick, rebuking hypocrisy, pleading for faith—this was Christ showing us the way of the Father, He who is "merciful and gracious, slow to anger, long-suffering and full of goodness."[4] In His life and especially in His death, Christ was declaring, "This is God's compassion I am showing you, as well as my own." In the perfect Son's manifestation of the perfect Father's care, in Their mutual suffering and shared sorrow for the sins and heartaches of the rest of us, we see ultimate meaning in the declaration: "For God so loved the world, that he gave his only begotten Son, that whosoever believeth in him should not perish, but have everlasting life. For God sent not his Son into the world to condemn the world; but that the world through him might be saved" (John 3:16–17).

I bear personal witness of a personal, living God, who knows our names, hears and answers prayers, and cherishes us eternally as children of His spirit. I testify that amidst the wondrously complex tasks inherent in the universe, He seeks our individual happiness and safety above all other godly concerns. We are created in His very image and likeness (see Genesis 1:26–27; Moses 2:26–27), and Jesus of Nazareth, His Only Begotten Son in the flesh, came to earth as the perfect mortal manifestation of His grandeur. In addition to the witness of the ancients we also have the modern miracle of Palmyra, the appearance of God the Father and His Beloved Son, the Savior of the world, to the boy prophet Joseph Smith. I testify of that appearance, and in the words of that prophet I, too, declare: "Our heavenly Father is more liberal in His views, and boundless in His mercies and blessings, than we are ready to believe or receive. . . . God does not look on sin with [the least degree of] allowance, but . . . the nearer we get to our heavenly Father, the more we are disposed

Amidst the wondrously complex tasks inherent in the universe, He seeks our individual happiness and safety above all other godly concerns.

to look with compassion on perishing souls; we feel that we want to take them upon our shoulders, and cast their sins behind our backs."[5]

I bear witness of a God who has such shoulders. And in the spirit of the holy apostleship, I reiterate as did one who held this office anciently: "Herein [then] is love, not that we loved God, but that he loved us, and sent his Son to be the propitiation for our sins. Beloved, if God so loved us, we ought also to love one another" (1 John 4:10–11)—and to love Him forever, I pray.

NOTES

From a talk given at general conference, October 2003.

1. Joseph Smith, *History of The Church of Jesus Christ of Latter-day Saints,* 7 vols. (Salt Lake City: The Church of Jesus Christ of Latter-day Saints, 1932–1952), 6:305.
2. Joseph Smith, *Lectures on Faith* (Salt Lake City: Deseret Book, 1985), lecture 3, paragraphs 4, 20.
3. See William Barclay, *The Mind of Jesus* (New York: Harper, 1961), especially the chapter "Looking at the Cross" for a discussion of this modern tendency.
4. *Lectures on Faith,* lecture 3, paragraph 20.
5. *Teachings of the Prophet Joseph Smith,* sel. Joseph Fielding Smith (Salt Lake City: Deseret Book, 1976), 257, 240–41.

INDEX

C

D

L

M

N

O

P

Packer, Boyd K., on starving deer, 62
Parents: children's faith affected by,
16–22; can protect children,
135–36
Perfection, in our words, 67
Persecution, Saints comforted
during, 85–86
Pioneers: of Hole-in-the-Rock
Expedition, 99–102; of Muddy
Mission, 103–6; faith of, 107–10;
call to action to rescue, 173
Plan of salvation: prophets teach,
147–48; role of Atonement in,
203–5
Pornography: children and, 128–29;
taking realistic views about,
129–31; fighting back against,
131–37
Potatoes, 77–78
Power, pornography and, 129–30
Pratt, Parley P., leads expedition,
99–100
Prayer: for children, 15–16; for
missionaries, 75–76; of Abraham
Lincoln, 111–12, 118; for
enemies, 115–18
Premortal Council, 203–5
Priesthood: worthiness for, 49–52;
restoration of, 154–55, 178–79; as
distinguishing feature of Church,
176–77; lost during apostasy,
177–78; divine authority and,
179–80; blessings of, 180–82
Priests, 152
Priorities, tithing indicates, 124–25
Prophets: see last days, 90–92;
Restoration and, 147–48; are
called of Jesus Christ, 163–65;
conference declares existence of,
172–73

Protestant Reformation, 152, 166–67
Providence, Rhode Island, 165–66
Punta Arenas Chile Stake, 195–96

R

Rasmus, Carolyn, 170–71
Reformation, 152, 166–67
Repentance: drawing unto Jesus
Christ through, 5–6; as
conditional gift of Atonement,
203–4
Restoration, 153–56; preparation for,
152–53; three things to focus on
in, 157–61; revelation and,
167–69; of priesthood, 178–79
Resurrection, 34, 204
Retention, 197
Returned missionary, learns
importance of personal
worthiness, 49–52
Revelation: apostasy and, 148–51;
Reformists' belief in continuing,
166–67; Joseph Smith and,
167–69; scriptures and
continuing, 184–90
Rogers, Fred, 108–9
Rowling, J. K., 135
Russia Moscow Mission, 77–78

S

Sacrament, corruption of, 151–52
Sacrifice: for missionary work,
78–79; of missionaries, 193–94
Safety, as blessing of tithing, 123–24
Saint Teresa Benedicta, 115–16
San Juan Mission, 99–102
Sandburg, Carl, on babies, 22

Satan: tithing provides safety from, 123–24; tempts in all dispensations, 148–51
Scriptures: continuing revelation and, 184–90; separate Godhead described in, 210–11
Second Coming, 81–85, 92–94
Self-criticism, 70–71
Self-doubt, 48–49
Senior missionaries, 77–78, 194–95
September 11, 2001, 81
Skepticism, 18
Smith, Belle, 102–3, 107, 109
Smith, Joseph: on living up to privileges, 42; author's testimony of, 46; on words, 66; on importance of preaching gospel, 80; God and Jesus Christ appear to, 153–54; on interest in building Zion, 156; testifying of, 157–59; revelation and, 167–69; restoration of priesthood and, 178; on priesthood as article of faith, 179; on arguments over Bible, 187; on knowing God, 216
Smith, Joseph F., pleads for children, 28
Smith, Joseph Stanford, 102–3, 109
Smith, Mary Fielding, 123
St. George, expedition to, 99–100
Stake president, has bike, 195
Starving deer, 62
Stein, Edith, 115–16

T

Talmage, James E.: on women, 42; on tithing, 125–26
Taylor, John: on ineffective teaching, 62; establishes San Juan Mission,

101; on revelation, 167; on Atonement, 206–7
Teachers, 58–64
Technology, 90
Teenage granddaughter, 40
Temples: increase in number of, 89; appreciating closeness of, 195–96
Terrorism, 81–85
Testimony: sharing, with children, 18–19, 21–22; of author, 46, 95–96, 189–90, 212–14; of Joseph Smith, 159; of God and Jesus Christ, 159–61, 220–21
Thanksgiving, 111–12
Thompson, Robert B., on Heber C. Kimball's departure, 180–81
Thoughts, negative, 70–71
Tithing, five reasons to pay, 122–26
Tongue, 67
Trials: overcoming, through Jesus Christ, 3–5, 7–8; of young mothers, 26–27; strengthening faith to endure, 108–9; exercising faith during, 140–41
Trinity, 208–11

V

Verbal abuse, 68–69
Vigilance, 134–35
Vineyard, 150–51
Violin, 193–94

W

Wedding feast, 94–95
Wesley, Charles, on priesthood with divine authority, 179–80
Whining, 71

Whitney, Orson F.: on negativity, 70;
    dream of, 200–201; on
    Atonement, 207
Wife, using kind words with, 68–69
Williams, Roger, 165–66
Witness, of Jesus Christ, 73–80
Women: divine nature of, 41–42;
    modesty and, 42–44; body image
    and, 44–46
Woodruff, Wilford, on overcoming
    fear and anxiety, 87–88
Words, 66–72
Worthiness, for priesthood, 49–52

Y

Young, Brigham, gives call to action,
    173

Young women: divine nature of,
    41–42; modesty and, 42–44; body
    image and, 44–46
Youth: self-doubt and, 48–49;
    personal worthiness of, 49–52;
    nurturing, 62–64. *See also* Young
    women

Z

Zion, Joseph Smith on interest in
    building, 156